Healthy, West African &Wise™ Food Guide

Healthy, West African &Wise™ Food Guide

Angela Tella, RD

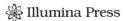 Illumina Press

This edition first published in the UK in 2010 by
Illumina Press
Petworth Way
RM12

Cover and interior design: Multimedia Styles
Editor: Ben Robertson
Photographer: John Uche
Production: S4E Media

A CIP record for this book is available at the British Library.

ISBN 978-0-9566660-1-7

Printed and bound in India by Print Vision

Contents

Also available from the same author

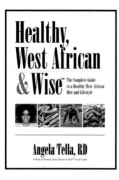

Healthy, West African & Wise™ - The Complete Guide to a Healthy West African Diet and Lifestyle.

Written by an expert in the field of nutrition and health, this unique book is the first ever diet and lifestyle book written specifically for West Africans, and provides tailored solutions to the diet- and lifestyle-related health issues facing people of West African origin today.

It shares important information about:

- Why chronic health conditions such as diabetes, obesity and hypertension are becoming increasingly common in people of West African origin.
- What you can do to prevent and manage these conditions.
- How West African foods can be part of a healthy balanced diet.
- How to avoid cultural stumbling blocks to good health.
- Healthy tips for cooking the foods you love and tips for healthy and savvy shopping.
- Making healthier choices when eating out - no matter the cuisine.
- Practical advice for overcoming barriers to being physically active.

PLUS...

- Sample recipes with nutritional analysis.
- Portion size guides for West African foods...and much, much more.

Introduction

Little has been documented about the nutritional qualities and health benefits of West African foods, yet an emerging body of research is beginning to highlight the amazing properties of foods consumed on a regular basis within the West African diet. The *Healthy West African & Wise™ Food Guide* is a companion to my first book, *Healthy, West African & Wise™ – The Complete Guide to a Healthy West African Diet and Lifestyle,* and aims to provide some much needed information on the nutritional and health benefits of 80 different West African foods. For each food, there are both scientific and English names as well as common names in many West African languages. For easy identification, pictures have been included too and where West African names have been unavailable, these should more than suffice. This book will present you with some remarkable facts about the foods eaten regularly as part of the West African diet. It is my hope that it will empower you to eat better today for a healthier tomorrow, while on your journey to becoming Healthy, West African and Wise. Enjoy!!

Angela Tella

Yam (Dioscorea rotundata and Dioscorea alata)

Francophone West Africa: Igname.

Sierra Leone: Nyam (Krio).

Nigeria: Ji (Igbo), Doya (Hausa), Isu (Yoruba).

Gambia: Nyami (Wolof), Yambi (Mende); Dadandingo, Dandingo (Mandinka).

Ghana: Bayere (Twi).

Cameroon: Yono (Bakweri).

Yams are a very versatile and important staple ingredient in West African cuisine. They are fried, boiled, roasted, mashed and even grated. Grated, seasoned water yams are made into small balls and cooked in seasoned stock to form dumplings or *ikokore*, a popular dish eaten in south-western Nigeria. Yams are also used commercially to make a variety of products such as yam flour, which is more convenient for making *pounded yam* - a firm, slightly sticky mass that is eaten with a soup or stew. The production of commercially prepared pounded yam was first attempted in Ivory Coast in the mid-1960s. Known by the trade name *Foutoupret*, it was produced by air-drying pre-cooked, grated or mashed yam. Parboiled yam chips are sun-dried and ground into flour known as *elubo*, which in turn is used to make *amala* – a dish very popular amongst the Yoruba.

Nutrition facts:

Yams are a source of dietary fibre, which is known to prevent constipation and help maintain good bowel health. They are a good source of phosphorus, and contain potassium, which is known to help reduce blood pressure levels. Yellow versions of yam contain beta-carotene, which the body uses to make vitamin A. One-pot recipes such as *yam pottage* (also known as *asaro* or *ebbeh*), are good ways of capturing any nutrients that may leach out during cooking.

Did you know that...?

There are over 150 species of yam grown throughout the world. Some species of yam naturally contain chemicals used to manufacture steroids and hormones used in oral birth-control tablets.

Plantain (Musa paradisiaca)

Ivory Coast, Mali and Gabon: Aloko.
Ghana: Bodie, Koko (Twi).
Nigeria: Ogede (Yoruba and Igbo), Agade (Hausa).
Cameroon: Planti (Bakweri).
Sierra Leone: Plantan, Plantin, Ogede (Krio).

A close relative of the banana, plantains can be used for cooking at any stage of ripeness. Ripe plantains are favoured by both adults and children alike, and can be fried, boiled, and roasted. In addition, unripe plantain can be sun-dried, ground to a flour and used to make a stiff dough or *fufu* which is eaten with soup or stew. Plantains, (usually ripe), are used to make *plantain chips*, a really popular West African snack. One variation of this is *kelewele,* a Ghanaian snack of ripe, diced or sliced plantain, marinated in delicious caramelised cloves, onions, garlic and hot pepper, and then fried. A popular Ivorian plantain side dish is *aloko* - plantains fried in palm oil and served with chilli and onion.

Nutrition facts:

Plantains are highly nutritious, containing large amounts of minerals such as phosphorus and calcium which are needed for healthy bones and teeth. They also contain potassium and are a good source of iron, as well as the antioxidant vitamins A and C.

Did you know that...?

Just like its cousin the banana, as a plantain ripens, its color changes from green to yellow to black. It also becomes sweeter due to the starch changing into naturally occurring sugars. As such, unripe plantains have a lower glycaemic index (GI) compared to ripe plantains, meaning that they slowly release their energy, ensuring more stable blood glucose (and therefore energy) levels.

Cassava (Manihot esculenta)

Francophone West Africa: Manioc.

Gambia: Nyambo, Mandioka banta nyambo (Mandinka).

Benin Republic: Akasa (Fon).

Senegal: Nambi (Wolof).

Guinea: Bantamyambi (Badyara).

Nigeria: Ege (Yoruba), Akpu (Igbo), Rogo (Hausa).

Ghana: Bankye (Twi).

Togo: Agbeli (Gbe-Vhe), Akobete (Yoruba).

Sierra Leone: Kasada (Krio).

Cameroon: Makpwamba (Douala).

Cassava is a well-known staple in West African cuisine and is eaten in a variety of ways. It can be boiled, fried, roasted, oven-baked and processed into a number of fermented food products like *fufu* (a smooth-textured, creamy-white cooked dough), *garri* or *farina* (grated cassava which is dry-fried or toasted and has a texture similar to dry couscous), and *attieke* (grated cassava which is steamed instead of toasted and has the texture of rehydrated couscous).

There are two varieties of cassava – the smaller, sweet varieties can be simply peeled and cooked before eating, whilst the larger, bitter varieties need elaborate processing to remove the naturally present and potentially toxic cyanide. Processing involves soaking peeled cassava in water for about 3-4 days, during which fermentation takes place.

Cassava flour (known as *lafun* in Nigeria and *kokonte* in Ghana) is a fibrous, coarse flour made by milling fermented, sun-dried cassava pieces.

Nutrition facts:

Cassava roots are very rich in starch, and contain significant amounts of potassium, fibre, calcium, phosphorus and vitamin C.

Did you know that...?

Cassava plants can grow as tall as or even taller than a human being and it is believed that former Brazilian slaves, who returned to West Africa in 1840, taught the *garri*-making process to West Africans.

Sweet Potato (Ipomoea batatas)

Francophone West Africa: Patate douce.

Nigeria: Dankeli (Hausa), Ji bekee (Igbo), Kukundunkun (Yoruba).

Gambia: Patat, Patato (Mandinka).

Ghana: Abrodewemaa (Twi).

Senegal: Pataas (Wolof).

Ivory Coast: Tingo (Baule).

Togo: Anango (Tem).

Liberia: Kwiso (Mano).

Sierra Leone: Pehtehteh, Kukunduku (Krio).

Cameroon: Ekpangu (Bakweri), Mabong (Long, Bafou); Ndoko (Kpe, Koosi, Wovea).

Known for their characteristic sweetness, sweet potatoes are a popular staple in West Africa, though they are not indigenous to West Africa. They can be boiled, fried or roasted, and are used in both savoury and sweet dishes such as *sweet potato pone,* a popular Liberian dessert dish.

Nutrition facts:

Sweet potatoes are particularly high in fibre and are a good source of vitamin C. Orange varieties contain significant amounts of beta-carotene, which the body converts to vitamin A, a powerful antioxidant. Sweet potatoes also have a low GI or glycaemic index, meaning that the natural sugars (and therefore energy) in them are released more slowly into the bloodstream.

Did you know that...?

In South America, the juice of red sweet potatoes is combined with lime juice to make a dye for cloth.

Cocoyam (Xanthosoma sagittifolium)

(Also known as Tannia, Elephant's ear, Taro potato and Yautia).
Nigeria: Ede (Igbo), Koko (Yoruba), Gwaza (Hausa).
Sierra Leone: Koko (Krio), Yabere (Mandinka, Fula-pulaar).
Ghana: Mankani (Twi).
Benin Republic: Mankani, Bangani (Bariba, Cotafon); Ikoko (Holly).
Senegal: Makabo.
Togo: Mankani (Gbe-vhe).
Cameroon: Ndaa (Kpe, Wovea); Ibokoko (Bakweri), Makabo (Long).

Cocoyams are similar to yams and are related to taro (*Colocasia esculentum*), a staple in South Pacific diets. In West African cuisine, cocoyams are peeled, boiled, mashed and added to soups as a thickening agent. They can also be fried, boiled and eaten just like yam. In Cameroon, cocoyam is made into balls and cooked with additional ingredients. This is known as *epankoko* and is very similar to Nigerian *ikokore*. The young leaves (known as *kontonmire* in Ghana) and flowers of the cocoyam plant are also eaten and used to prepare traditional soups.

Nutrition facts:

Cocoyams are rich in carbohydrate and so make a good energy source. They also contain calcium and phosphorus, both needed for healthy bones and teeth,

and iron, an important component of haemoglobin. Cocoyam leaves contain silicate crystals which can irritate the throat and other internal body linings if not cooked properly.

Did you know that...?

Cocoyam is hypoallergenic, making it a suitable food for anyone with allergies. It is also easily digestible due to its relatively small starch grains.

Tiger Nuts (Cyperus esculentus)

(Also known as Earth nuts, Earth almonds and Rush Nuts).
Gambia: Garamanti (Mandinka), Ndere (Wolof).
Nigeria: Ofio (Yoruba), Aki Awusa (Igbo), Ayaa (Hausa).
Ghana: Atadwe (Twi).
Mali: Njoro, Nton (Manding- Bambara).
Niger: Hanti (Songhai).
Senegal: Nder (Wolof), Epaympay (Diola).
Togo: Amo (Tem), Nansacha (Dagbani).
Ivory Coast: Toro, Tchoro (Manding-Dyula); Toki (Manding-Maninka).
Sierra Leone: Gramanti, Kramantin, Taiganoht (Krio).

Tiger nuts are a daily ingredient in the diets of North Africans and are also popular in Spain, where they are known as *chufa*. Originally a native of the Mediterranean, tiger nuts grow well in warm climates such as in West Africa where they are eaten mainly as a snack. The Hausa of northern Nigeria and Ghana make tiger nut 'milk' by finely grinding the nuts and straining the liquid from them. This is then boiled with flour and sugar to make a custard-like dessert.

Nutrition facts:

Tiger nuts consist mainly of starch and fat of which 75% is monounsaturated fat. They are also a rich source of dietary fibre, containing 19g of fibre in 100g of nuts.

In addition, tiger nuts are high in potassium, which has been proven to reduce blood pressure levels. They are also a good source of phosphorus and antioxidant vitamins C and E, as well as a rich source of linoleic acid.

Did you know that...?

A tiger nut is not really a nut but a tuber. In addition to being eaten as a snack, tiger nuts can be made into flour and contain a pleasantly flavoured oil which is extracted for a range of uses. In the Mediterranean, tiger nuts are used to make desserts, ice cream and even beverages.

Garden Egg (Solanum aethiopicum L.) and Bitter Tomato (Solanum incanum L.)

(Also known as African eggplant).

Francophone West Africa: Aubergine Africaine.

Nigeria: Asun, Ikan, Igba (Yoruba); Afufa, Anara (Igbo); Gauta (Hausa).

Togo: Gboma.

Benin Republic: Gboma (Fon, Tchabe).

Sierra Leone: Jackato, Jiblohks, Kohbohkohboh (Krio).

Gambia: Jahato (Wolof); Jarto, Jakato, Jehato (Mandinka).

Sengal: Jaxato (Wolof).

Ghana: Nnuadewa, Ntrowa (Twi).

Cameroon: Jagatu.

Liberia: Bitter balls, County pepper.

Garden eggs are one of the most commonly eaten fruit vegetables in tropical Africa, and are closely related to the aubergine. Garden eggs are eaten raw (skin included), or cooked in a variety of vegetable, meat, or fish stews and sauces. Some varieties are bitter to taste (earning them the name 'bitter tomato'), but many are sweet or bland, especially when harvested young. They are also used as a meat substitute because their spongy texture easily absorbs flavour from other foods and when chewed, they provide a mouth-feel similar to that of meat.

Their leaves can be eaten as a leafy vegetable and are especially important in south-eastern Nigeria and in Cameroon.

Nutrition facts:

Garden eggs are high in fibre and low in calories and sodium. They are a good potassium source and contain calcium and iron too. Additionally, garden eggs contain moderate amounts of beta-carotene, B vitamins, and vitamin C. They have small amounts of protein with significant amounts of methionine, one of the essential amino acids rarely found in plant-based foods.

Did you know that...?

Some types of garden egg leaves have high and potentially toxic solanine content - this is rendered harmless by cooking.

Bitter Leaf (Vernonia amygdalina)

Nigeria: Ewuro (Yoruba); Onugbu, Olugbu (Igbo); Shiwaka (Hausa); Atidot (Efik).
Ghana: Awonyono (Twi).
Cameroon: Ndo.
Sierra Leone: Bita Lif, Bitas (Krio).
Benin Republic: Eyouro (Holly), Aloman (Fon, Cotafon, Mahi).

The characteristic bitter taste of this popularly eaten leafy vegetable is what makes it unique. It is used fresh or dried in a number of West African soups and stews, such as Cameroonian *ndole*. Prior to use, the leaves are bruised and washed several times to get rid of some of their bitter taste. In some parts of West Africa, unprocessed leaves are eaten raw mixed with salt and palm oil.

Nutrition facts:

Bitter leaf is an excellent source of fibre and contains small amounts of phosphorous and selenium. It provides some vitamin C and is also a good source of iron. Dried bitter leaf is rich in phytochemicals, which are known to have antioxidant properties, protecting the body against free-radical damage.

Did you know that...?

Bitter leaf juice is traditionally used to treat wounds in a similar way to iodine, and is said to be just as effective.

Bush Okra (Corchorus olitorius)

(Also known as West African Sorrel, Jew's Mallow, Tossa Jute, Long-fruited Jute and Vegetable Jute).

Francophone West Africa: Oseille de Guinee.

Benin Republic: Ademe (Cotafon), Ayoyo (Ife), Ninnouwi (Fon).

Togo: Ademe.

Nigeria: Ewedu (Yoruba); Lalo (Hausa); Arira, Ahuhara (Igbo).

Senegal: Akud, Bot a nay (Serer); Mbali, Kren-kren (Wolof).

Gambia: Krain-krain, Kereng-kereng (Wolof).

Sierra Leone: Kren-kren, Kirinkirin (Krio).

Ghana: Ayoyo.

Cameroon: Crain-crain.

Bush okra is a popular leafy vegetable in Nigeria, Ivory Coast, Benin Republic and Cameroon. When cooked, it has a mucilaginous quality similar to that of okra. Bush okra can be used either fresh or dried and is commonly used in the preparation of *palava soup,* a vegetable soup thickened with powdered melon seeds. *Palava soup* is also popularly known as *egusi soup.*

Nutrition facts:

Bush okra is high in fibre, important for bowel health, as well as calcium and iron. It is also rich in antioxidants in the form of vitamin C and beta-carotene, which the body converts into vitamin A.

Did you know that...?

Some types of *corchorus olitorius* are grown for the production of jute fabric, a coarse fabric used as an important packaging material. Jute fabric is also used in the manufacture of environmentally friendly (or eco-friendly) bags.

Cassava Leaves (Manihot esculenta)

Francophone West Africa: Feuilles de manioc.

Nigeria: Rogo (Hausa); Mushu, Ipoto, Mpoto (Igbo).

Gambia: Nyambi jambo (Mandinka).

Sierra Leone: Kasada lif (Krio).

Cameroon: Nkwem (Ewondo).

Ghana: Bankye Ahahen (Twi).

Benin Republic: Finyin (Fon, Mahi).

Liberia: Cassava greens.

Cassava leaves are a popular vegetable, especially in Sierra Leone and Liberia, where they are used to prepare soups and stews. Naturally poisonous due to their cyanide content, cassava leaves are cooked after being washed and finely shredded. Boiling or stewing renders the cyanide harmless.

Nutrition facts:

Cassava leaves are a very significant source of dietary protein, with a protein quality similar to that found in chicken eggs, the gold standard for measuring protein quality. They are also a good source of vitamins A and C.

Did you know that...?

Cassava leaves contain between five to twenty times more cyanide than cassava roots, but have a greater ability to rapidly lose it during cooking.

Red Sorrel (Hibiscus sabdariffa)

(Also known as Roselle, Sour leaf and Guinea sorrel).

Gambia: Sour-sour (Aku); Domoda, Kucha, Dawonjo (Mandinka); Bisab (Wolof).

Nigeria: Ishapa (Yoruba).

Ghana: Suule (Hausa).

Sierra Leone: Sawa, Sawa-sawa, Sohrel (Krio).

Benin Republic: Sinko (Fon), Kpakpa (Tchabe).

Red Sorrel is a leafy vegetable commonly found all over West Africa. Its fresh, tender leaves and stalks are naturally sour and are eaten as salad and as a pot herb. Washing the leaves several times before use reduces its distinct sour taste.

Nutrition facts:

Red sorrel is rich in iron, calcium and vitamin C, and is an excellent source of beta-carotene, which the body converts into vitamin A. It is also a good source of vitamins B_1 (thiamin), B_2 (riboflavin) and B_3 (niacin).

Did you know that...?

Red sorrel flowers are used to make a popular, refreshing West African hibiscus tea that can be drunk hot or cold. Shown to have anti-hypertensive effects, this tea is known by a variety of names: *bissap* in Senegal, *wanjo juice* in Gambia, *dabilenni* in Mali, *karkanji* in Chad and *zobo* in northern Nigeria.

Fluted Pumpkin Leaves (Telfaria occidentalis)

(Also known as Fluted pumpkin, Fluted gourd and Telfairia nut).

Nigeria: Ugu (Igbo); Ganye kabewa (Hausa); Iroko, Aporoko (Yoruba), Ubong (Efik).

Cameroon: Okongobong, Okongebong.

Sierra Leone: Oroko (Krio).

Benin Republic: Roko, Iroko (Holly); Loko (Fon, Mahi).

Fluted pumpkin leaves are well known for their pleasant taste and are used in a variety of soups and stews. The tender shoots of the fluted pumpkin plant are also eaten and its oily seeds have lactating properties. Consequently, they are widely consumed by nursing mothers as a means of improving the quality and volume of breast milk. Also, the Yoruba communities of Benin Republic use fluted pumpkin seeds to make a Beninoise dish known as *avlouda*.

Nutrition facts:

Fluted pumpkin leaves are high in fibre and are a rich source of folic acid, and vitamins A, C and K. They also contain calcium, zinc, potassium, cobalt, copper, and iron, all important minerals for good health. Due to its high iron content, fluted pumpkin leaf juice is traditionally used to treat anaemia. Its high vitamin C content enhances this benefit, as vitamin C is known to aid the absorption of iron.

Did you know that...?

The scientific name of the fluted pumpkin is derived from the name of Charles Telfair, the famous Irish naturalist, botanist and plant collector.

African Spinach (Amaranthus cruentus and Amaranthus caudatus)

Francophone West Africa: Amaranthe.

Ghana: Asibe (Twi), Alefu (Hausa).

Sierra Leone: Grins (Krio), Hondi (Mende), Boroboro (Fula-pulaar).

Nigeria: Efo tete (Yoruba); Alayyafu, Alayyaho (Hausa); Inyan afia (Efik), Inine (Igbo).

Gambia: Morongo, Beremba (Mandinka); Boroboro (Wolof), Mboum (Aku).

Guinea: Fondulo (Kissi), Boro (Mandinka), Boron (Maninka).

Benin Republic: Fotete (Tchabe), Tete (Mahi).

Guinea Bissau: Bredo (Crioula).

Mali: Boron (Bambara).

Senegal: Bura bura ba (Manding-Bambara), Mbuma (Serer).

Cameroon: Green.

Different varieties of African spinach are widely eaten in the Western region of Africa. *Amaranthus cruentus* for example is popular in Togo, Benin Republic and Sierra Leone, where its leaves are added to soups and stews or eaten as a side dish. *Amaranthus caudatus* is both eaten and grown for ornamental purposes.

Nutrition facts:

Compared to other leafy vegetables, African spinach is extraordinarily high in vitamin A, vitamin C, folic acid, iron and calcium. Also, depending on the particular species, it contains exceptional amounts of good quality protein (between 27-30% protein on a dry weight basis).

Did you know that...?

In colonial times, African spinach was recommended to Europeans living in Africa as the best substitute for spinach.

Baobab Leaves (Adansonia digitata)

Senegal & Niger: Boki, Bokki (Fulani).

Ivory Coast: Sira (Manding-dioula).

Guinea-Bissau: Cabaceira, Calabaceira (Crioulo).

Ghana: Odadie (Twi), Tua (Nankani).

Nigeria: Luru, Kuka (Hausa); Bokki (Fulani).

Gambia: Naa (Mandinka); Sita, Bui, Lalo (Wolof).

Sierra Leone: Sida, Gbowulo.

Benin Republic: Kpassa (Fon, Mahi).

Favoured for their ability to thicken soups, baobab leaves are a major food of the Hausa-speaking peoples of West Africa. Young leaves are sun-dried and ground into a powder before use. Baobab leaf soup (*miyan kuka* in Nigeria), is also commonly known across West Africa by the Wolof name of *lalo*.

Nutrition facts:

Dried baobab leaves are a good protein source and contain adequate amounts of six of the eight essential amino acids. They have a very high level of beta-carotene and are also a significant source of calcium, magnesium, manganese, potassium, phosphorus, iron, sodium and zinc.

Did you know that...?

Bark stripped from the baobab tree can be made into rope and even clothing.

Sweet Potato Leaves (Ipomoea batatas)

Sierra Leone: Pehtehteh lif (Krio).

Liberia: Potato greens.

Gambia: Patat (Wolof), Patato (Mandinka).

Mali: Saga saga.

Benin Republic: Douki (Mahi).

Sweet potato leaves are very popular in Guinea, Gambia, Liberia and Sierra Leone, where young leaves and vine tips of leaves are widely consumed as a vegetable. They have a mild, dense flavour and can be eaten raw. Sweet potato leaves feature in a number of West African sauces including Malinese *saga saga sauce* and Burkinabe *sauce feuille*, which also contains groundnuts.

Nutrition facts:

Sweet potato leaves and shoots are a rich source of beta-carotene which the body converts into vitamin A, a powerful antioxidant with the ability to protect the body against free-radical damage. They also contain vitamin B_2 (riboflavin) and vitamin C, and have a relatively high fibre content.

Did you know that...?

Sweet potato leaves are normally ready for harvest from 40 days after planting. Young leaves can be repeatedly harvested from then on as long as a significant proportion of fully developed leaves are left on the plant.

Waterleaf (Talinum fruticosum and Talinum triangulare Willd)

(Also known as Surinam spinach and Lagos bologi).

Nigeria: Gbure (Yoruba), Ngbolodi (Igbo).

Gambia: Bologi, Hop (Wolof); Bologi (Aku); Boronoro (Mandinka).

Sierra Leone: Legos bologi (Krio).

Liberia: Water greens.

Benin Republic: Goure (Yoruba), Tokpede fonton (Fon).

Ghana: Bokoboko (Twi).

Cameroon: Boloki, Mboloki (Bakweri).

Popular throughout the tropics, waterleaf is a fleshy and semi-succulent herb with tiny pink flowers. Its taste and slimy texture when cooked makes it an important ingredient of *edikaikong,* a soup consisting of a variety of different leafy vegetables, which is particularly favoured by the Efik-speaking tribes of south-eastern Nigeria. A similar dish is also eaten in Cameroon.

Nutrition facts:

Not surprisingly, waterleaf is almost 91% water. It is low in fibre and contains good amounts of beta-carotene, which the body converts into vitamin A - it therefore possesses antioxidant properties. Waterleaf also contains high amounts of oxalate, and so should be avoided or eaten in small amounts by those suffering from gout, kidney disorders and rheumatoid arthritis. That said, blanching or cooking removes nearly half of the soluble oxalate.

Did you know that...?

Waterleaf contains pectinase, a naturally occurring enzyme with a softening ability, explaining its use to soften coarser leaves in vegetable soups in some parts of West Africa.

African Jointfir Leaves (Gnetum africanum and Gnetum buchholzianum)

Nigeria: Ukazi, Okazi (Igbo); Afang (Efik and Ibibio).
Gabon: Nkumu (Fang).
Cameroon: Okok (Fang), Ikoko (Douala), Eru.

Harvested from the African jointfir, a climbing vine that grows in the wild, these dark green leaves are usually finely shredded and cooked in soups and stews, though they can also be eaten raw as a salad. Both species are similar, though *Gnetum africanum* is more readily available and therefore more popularly eaten. The main difference between the two species is that *Gnetum africanum* has thinner, much paler leaves than *Gnetum buchholzianum*.

Nutrition facts:

African jointfir leaves are high in fibre and contain all eight of the essential amino acids, making them a good source of protein (16.5% dry weight). They are also rich in iron and vitamin C.

Did you know that...?

African jointfir leaves are chewed to cure hangovers, as they are said to ease the effects of drunkenness. They are also used as an antidote for venomous stings and bites.

Lagos Spinach (Celosia argentea)

(Also known as Quail grass and Lizard bean).

Francophone West Africa: Celosie argentee.

Nigeria: Soko (Yoruba), Farar alayafu (Hausa).

Sierra Leone: Sohkohtoh-yohkohtoh (Krio), An-kokoro (Temne), Yogoto (Mende).

Ghana: Nkywodue (Akan Fante), Sokoto (Mano).

Liberia: Boh (Mano).

Senegal: Ngo ban ku (Manding–Bambara).

Benin Republic: Tchokoyokoto (Ife, Yoruba); Alefo (Bariba, Kotokoli); Soman (Fon, Mahi).

A relative of the African spinach family, these nutty-flavoured leaves are steamed and eaten as a side dish or cooked in soups or stews. This traditional vegetable is found throughout tropical Africa but is extremely popular in southern Benin Republic and also amongst the Yoruba of south-western Nigeria, where it is known as *soko yokoto* (translated, make husbands fat) or *soko* for short. It is also popular in Togo, Ghana and Cameroon.

Nutrition facts:

Lagos spinach is particularly rich in iron and calcium and its young leaves are especially rich in beta-carotene and vitamin C. It is also a rich source of protein. As with all vegetables, brief cooking helps to preserve the nutritional content of this vegetable.

Did you know that...?

Lagos spinach is closely related to another *celosia* plant (known as Cock's comb), the flowers of which resemble a rooster's comb. Lagos spinach is also known as lizard bean, because the plant is often frequented by lizards.

Okra (Abelmoschus esculentus)

(Also known as Okro, Lady's finger and Ladies finger).

Francophone West Africa: Gombo.

Ghana: Nkruman, Nkruma (Twi).

Nigeria: Kubewa (Hausa), Okwuru (Igbo), Ila (Yoruba).

Senegal: Kanda, Kanja (Wolof).

Sierra Leone: Ohkroh (Krio).

Gambia: Kanjo (Mandinka); Kanjo gombo, Kanja (Wolof).

Cameroon: Okra, Gombo.

Benin Republic: Sinku (Fon), Ila (Tchabe).

The mucilaginous quality of okra makes it a popular soup vegetable in West Africa, where it is used to thicken soups and stews. Okra can be used fresh or as a powder made from dried pods. In addition, young whole okra pods are boiled, blanched, fried, sautéed, steamed and served as a side dish. The leaves of the okra plant are also eaten.

Nutrition facts:

Okra is high in both soluble and insoluble fibre. It is also a good source of beta-carotene, vitamin C, and minerals, such as calcium, magnesium, and potassium. Okra seeds contain good quantities of vegetable protein and about 40% oil, similar in quality to olive oil. Due to its high soluble fibre content, okra contributes to bowel health and can help lower cholesterol levels. Okra leaves are also nutritious, and provide protein, calcium, and iron, as well as vitamins A and C.

Did you know that...?
Dried okra powder is used commercially in the production of salad dressings, ice creams, cheese spreads, and even confectionery.

Sweet Pepper (Capsicum annuum)

(Also known as Bell Pepper).
Francophone West Africa: Piment doux, Poivron.
Gambia: Karni kittingo (Mandinka).
Senegal: Kaani-salaat, Kani tubab (Wolof).
Ghana: Moko (Twi).
Sierra Leone: Big pehpeh (Krio).

An essential ingredient in many West African dishes, notably *jollof rice* and red stews, sweet peppers have a range of culinary uses. In addition to being used as a cooking ingredient, sweet peppers can be eaten raw (for example in salads), and are often used as a garnish to add a colourful finishing touch to a range of dishes, including West African grilled fish dishes.

Nutrition facts:

Bursting with vitamins A and C, sweet peppers are also a good source of fibre. Just one pepper contains enough vitamin C to meet an adult's daily requirement of this vitamin, for almost two days.

Did you know that...?

Botanically speaking, a sweet pepper is actually a fruit rather than a vegetable, and is the only member of the *Capsicum* (pepper) family that does not produce capsaicin, the heat-producing chemical that gives peppers their fiery taste.

Coconut (Cocos nucifera)

Francophone West Africa: Noix de coco.
Gambia: Koko, Koka (Wolof); Tubab sibo (Mandinka).
Ghana: Kube (Twi).
Senegal: Koko (Wolof).
Nigeria: Agbon (Yoruba); Aku bekee (Igbo), Kwa kwa (Hausa).
Cameroon: Muangamulikawo (Bakweri).

The coconut is the fruit of the coconut palm and has a variety of uses in West African cuisine. The flesh is eaten as a snack, as well as grated to make coconut milk or cream for cooking. It is also used to make coconut oil, popularly used for cooking in Sierra Leone. Coconut water, the liquid naturally present in coconuts, makes a refreshing drink in the West African heat.

Nutrition facts:

Coconut is known for its high saturated fat content and this is reflected in its oil. It is high in potassium and has fair amounts of phosphorous and iron, as well as fibre. It contains smaller amounts of calcium, iron, magnesium, zinc, copper, manganese and selenium, as well as vitamins C and E.

Did you know that...?

Coconut water remains sterile until a coconut is opened. As it is of similar composition to blood plasma, it can be used in place of intravenous fluid during emergency transfusions. In India, coconut shells are used to make buttons.

Mango (Mangifera indica)

Nigeria: Mangoro (Yoruba, Igbo, Hausa).

Gambia: Mangoro (Wolof), Tubab duto (Mandinka).

Senegal: Mango (Wolof).

Benin Republic: Maga, Amaga (Fon).

Cameroon: Mangoro, Mangola (Bakweri).

Sierra Leone: Mangro (Krio).

Smooth and juicy with their own special flavour, mangoes are a popular West African fruit. They are eaten as a snack or as a dessert after meals. In Guinea, they are cooked or stewed with a little salt until mushy. A similar dish of stewed mango and cloves sweetened with corn syrup is commonly eaten in Liberia, as is *mango fool*, a chilled dessert dish of stewed mango and custard.

Nutrition facts:

Mangoes are high in prebiotic dietary fibre, which stimulates the growth of good bacteria in the gut and therefore contributes to bowel health. They are also rich in vitamin C, as well as beta-carotene, which the body converts to vitamin A. Mangoes are one of the few fruit sources of vitamin E, a potent antioxidant, and contain vitamin B_3 (niacin) and potassium. They also contain polyphenols, which have a protective effect against cancer.

Did you know that...?

Originating in India, there are over 1000 different varieties of mangoes through-

out the world.

African Pear (Dacryodes edulis G.don)

(Also known as African plum, Native pear, Bush butter and Butterfruit).

Francophone West Africa: Safou, Safoutier.

Nigeria: Ube (Igbo), Eben (Efik), Elemi (Yoruba), Ibe (Kalabari), Orumu (Urhobo).

Ivory Coast: Vi (Abe), Tsai (Akye), Kerandja (Anyi).

Benin Republic: Omunu.

Cameroon: Bosao (Douala); Boasu (Kpe).

The smooth, shiny purple skin of the African pear hides a light green fruit pulp which softens when roasted or boiled. The skin and and oily pulp can be eaten and the large seed discarded. The oily pulp has a bland, creamy flavour similar to that of avocado.

Nutrition facts:

African pear pulp contains between 33-66% oil, of which 58% is unsaturated, making it the only other fruit (besides the avocado) that is high in fat. It is also a good source of potassium and contains small amounts of sodium and carbohydrate. In addition, it contains between 9-12% protein with a good amino-acid balance, making it a good protein source. Also, African pear pulp is rich in beta-carotene which the body converts into vitamin A, and contains vitamins B_1 (thiamin), B_2 (riboflavin) and B_3 (niacin), as well as vitamins C, E, K and folic acid.

Did you know that...?

Due to its similarity in taste, composition and texture to the avocado, the term "africado" has been coined for the African pear and suggested for international marketing purposes.

Watermelon (Citrullus vulgaris)

Francophone West Africa: Pasteque.

Gambia: Saro (Mandinka).

Senegal: Xaal (Wolof).

Sierra Leone: Watamelon (Krio).

Cameroon: Esaka bawu (Bafok).

Togo: Kanjinga (Tem).

Watermelons are a popular, refreshing and delicious snack in the West African heat. They can be eaten on their own or as part of a fruit salad, and can even be juiced. Also, the black seeds embedded in the red, watery flesh are edible.

Nutrition facts:

Watermelons are 92% water, and are high in vitamin C and beta-carotene which the body converts into vitamin A, a powerful antioxidant. They also contain magnesium, potassium, calcium and phosphorous. Watermelons are a good source of lycopene, which is responsible for the red colour of watermelons and is known to have a protective effect against prostate cancer. What's more, watermelon seeds are a good source of essential fatty acids and protein.

Did you know that...?

The watermelon plant is closely related to the egusi plant. Both plants look so much alike that each can easily be mistaken for the other. Egusi gourds even look like small watermelons.

Sugar Cane (Sacchrum officinarum)

Francophone West Africa: Cane de sucre.

Nigeria: Reke (Hausa), Ireke (Yoruba), Achara mmako (Igbo).

Ghana: Ahwedee (Twi).

Sierra Leone: Shugaken (Krio).

Cameroon: Mokoko (Bakweri).

A popular snack throughout West Africa, sugar cane is chewed raw to extract its naturally sweet juice. In Liberia, sugar cane juice is fermented and distilled into Liberian rum, an alcoholic drink known by Liberians as *cane juice*. In northern Nigeria, sugar cane juice is used to sweeten *kunun zaki*, a popular non-alcoholic beverage made from sorghum and millet. Commercially, sugar cane juice is extracted and used to manufacture sugar.

Nutrition facts:

Sugar cane is primarily an energy source as it contains carbohydrate, in the form of natural sugars. It also contains small amounts of vitamin C, calcium, and iron.

Did you know that...?

Sugarcane is really a type of grass. It contains alpha hydroxy acids (AHAs), natural acids which are used in the formulation of skin care products. Additionally, sugar cane is used to produce ethanol, an alternative fuel which is more environmentally friendly than fossil fuels such as diesel and petrol.

Cashew Apple (Anacardium occidentale)

Francophone West Africa: Pomme de cajou.

Gambia: Casuo, Kasuwu (Mandinka); Dakasso, Darkasu (Wolof).

Nigeria: Kanju (Hausa), Kasu (Yoruba).

Benin Republic: Akaju, Lacazu (Fon); Kaju, Ekaju (Yoruba).

Senegal: Darkasa (Wolof).

Guinea: Somo (Malinke).

Sierra Leone: Kushu (Krio).

Popular in West Africa when in season, the cashew apple is actually a swollen stalk attaching the cashew nut to the cashew tree. Cashew apples are yellow or red when ripe and have a sweet, slightly sour taste. They must be eaten with care as their juice is well-known to irreversibly stain clothing. The cashew nut is the true fruit of the cashew tree and is a popular West African snack. In Gambia, cashew nuts are sometimes ground and used in place of groundnuts to thicken soups.

Nutrition facts:

Cashew apples are very high in vitamin C and are also low in calories. The nuts are a good protein source and are high in monounsaturated fat, which is known to lower cholesterol levels. In addition, cashew nuts contain good amounts of fibre, calcium, copper, magnesium and iron.

Did you know that...?

The shell surrounding the cashew nut contains a caustic resin which is carefully removed before the nut is eaten. The caustic resin is used in Gambia for tanning and tattooing. It is also used commercially to make varnishes and insecticides.

Baobab Fruit (Adansonia digitata)

(Also known as Monkey bread).

Senegal, Nigeria & Niger: Bokki.

Mali & Ivory Coast: Sira.

Burkina Faso: Sira ou nsira (Bambara), Toega (More).

Gambia: Sito (Mandinka), Bui (Wolof), Boki (Fula-pulaar).

Sierra Leone: Sida (Mandinka), Monki bred (Krio).

The hairy fruit of the baobab tree has a powdery pulp with a tangy, sweet and sour taste. It is used to make traditional drinks such as *bouyi* in Mali and *sitajio* in Gambia, and is an essential ingredient in *ngalakh*, a Senegalese dessert of millet couscous, flavoured with peanut butter. In Ghana, fermented baobab seeds are made into a condiment called *kantong*, used to flavour relishes and soups.

Nutrition facts:

The flesh of the baobab fruit is an excellent source of calcium, containing more than twice as much as milk. It has an exceptionally high amount of vitamin C (six times that of oranges), and contains soluble fibre with prebiotic qualities. Prebiotics help bowel health by promoting the growth of good bacteria.

Did you know that...?

In the UK and the US, powdered baobab fruit is now added to some foods such as smoothies, to enhance their flavour and to improve their nutritional qualities.

African Star Apple (Chrysophyllum albidum)

(Also known as White star apple).

Nigeria: Udara (Igbo), Agbalumo (Yoruba), Agwalugwa (Hausa).

Ghana: Akassa, Lassa (Adangme).

Sierra Leone: Tekene (Kono), Duauguli (Mende).

Benin Republic: Azongogwe, Azonbobwe (Fon, Yoruba, Nago).

The African star apple is a large berry which, when ripe, is orange-yellow in colour. Its succulent flesh which is eaten, surrounds five flattened, brown seeds arranged in a star shape. In some parts of West Africa, oil is extracted from the seeds and used for cooking or making soap.

Nutrition facts:

African star apples are a rich source of iron and contain an exceptionally high amount of vitamin C - 100 times that of oranges and 10 times that of guava. This is an excellent combination because vitamin C is known to enhance the absorption of iron in the body. They are also rich in potassium, and should therefore be eaten in small quantities by those with kidney problems. African star apples also contain calcium, small amounts of zinc, magnesium, phosphorous and copper.

Did you know that...?

The African star apple tree is part of the same family as the South American chicle tree, the original source of chewing gum.

Guava (Psidium guajava)

(Also known as Poor man's apple and Apple of the Tropics).

Gambia: Biabo (Mandinka), Biab (Wolof).

Nigeria: Gova (Igbo), Gwaabaa (Hausa), Woba (Efik).

Senegal: Guyaab (Wolof).

Guinea-Bissau: Guaiaba (Crioulo).

Benin Republic: Kenkun (Fon).

Sierra Leone: Gueva (Krio).

Guavas are a favourite tropical fruit widely eaten in West Africa. This highly fragrant fruit can be eaten raw or cooked and comes with flesh ranging in colour from a creamy white to a deep red. They have an aromatic, sweet-acid flavour and their high pectin content makes them suitable for jam and jelly-making.

Nutrition facts:

The guava is exceptionally high in vitamin C, containing five times the amount of vitamin C in oranges. Most of the vitamin C is found in the skin, followed by the firm flesh, and then in the pulp at the centre of the fruit. Guavas also contain iron, and beta-carotene, which the body converts into the antioxidant vitamin A. It is a good source of fibre, and also contains small amounts of vitamins B_1 (thiamin), B_2 (riboflavin) and B_3 (niacin).

Did you know that...?

Guava powder, containing between 2500-3000mg of vitamin C, was commonly added to military rations during World War II.

Banana (Musa sapientum)

Francophone West Africa: Banane.

Gambia: Banano (Mandinka), Banan (Wolof).

Guinea: Banema.

Nigeria: Ayaba (Hausa), Ogede were (Yoruba), Ogede (Igbo).

Benin Republic: Kwekwe (Fon).

Ghana: Kwedu (Twi).

Senegal: Banaana (Wolof).

Cameroon: Mbo (Bakweri).

If any fruit is synonymous with the tropics, then it has to be the banana. Well-known and eaten all over the world, the banana is a staple fruit in West Africa. Bananas can be eaten raw or cooked and are used as an ingredient in foods such as in Sierra Leonean *rice bread*. Their natural, easy-to-open packaging makes them highly convenient to eat on the go!

Nutrition facts:

Packed with potassium, which is known to lower blood pressure, bananas are a great source of fibre and B vitamins. Their low glycaemic index or GI means that bananas release their energy over a prolonged period, making them an excellent snack. They are also a good source of vitamins A and C.

Did you know that...?

Fermented, over-ripe bananas are used as a raising agent in large-scale bread-making. Growing up to 20 feet tall – as tall as a two-storey house - the banana plant is the largest plant on earth without a woody stem.

Pineapple (Ananas comosus)

Francophone West Africa: Ananas.
Sierra Leone: Painapul (Krio).
Ivory Coast: Ableble (Baule).
Ghana: Abrobe (Twi).
Nigeria: Arbarba (Hausa); Akwuozuzu, Akwu olu (Igbo); Ope oyinbo (Yoruba).
Benin Republic: Agonde.
Senegal: Sanaanaa (Wolof).
Cameroon: Liangi (Kpe, Wovea), Yijang (Bafok).

The pineapple is another fruit that is popular in West Africa. Originating from South America, pineapples are succulent, with a delicious flavour, making them a pleasant, refreshing snack. They are the major ingredient in Liberian *pineapple beer*, a non-alcoholic beverage.

Nutrition facts:

Pineapples contain fibre and have a very high vitamin C content. They are also a good source of manganese as well as vitamins B_1 (thiamin) and B_2 (riboflavin).

Did you know that...?

Raw pineapple contains bromelain, an enzyme which breaks down protein. Consequently, pineapple juice can be used as a marinade and tenderiser for meat.

Papaya (Carica papaya)

(Also known as Pawpaw).

Nigeria: Ibepe (Yoruba), Une ezi (Igbo), Gwanda (Hausa).

Gambia: Pakaia (Mandinka), Popokaiyo (Mandinka, Wolof).

Sierra Leone: Pohpoh (Krio).

Benin Republic: Kpen (Fon).

Ghana: Brofre (Twi).

Senegal: Paapaaya (Wolof).

Papaya is a commonly eaten fruit in West Africa and is a good addition to fruit salads. Papayas that are just beginning to show signs of ripening are cooked and eaten as a vegetable, and make a great accompaniment to meat dishes. Due to its high pectin content, the papaya is an important ingredient of Senegalese *papaya jam*. It is also used in Liberia to make *papaya tarts*.

Nutrition facts:

The papaya is an excellent source of vitamin C and beta-carotene, both of which possess antioxidants properties. It is also rich in fibre and is a good source of potassium, which is known to lower blood pressure. It also contains phosphorous, zinc, magnesium and iron.

Did you know that...?

Wrapping tough meat in papaya leaves softens it. This is due to the presence of an enzyme with the ability to break down protein. Known as papain, this enzyme is present in the sap and leaves of the papaya tree, and in the skins of raw, unripe papayas. Papain can also be used to wash clothes and remove stains, and to treat insect stings and kill intestinal worms.

Avocado (Persea americana)

(Also known as Butter pear and Alligator pear).

Francophone West Africa: Avocat.

Gambia: Pear, Ovocado (Mandinka, Wolof).

Sierra Leone: Bohta pia (Krio).

Nigeria: Pia (Yoruba), Ube bekee (Igbo).

Ghana: Paya (Twi, Adangme).

Cameroon: Pear.

With a smooth, buttery texture and mild, creamy taste, avocados are used in a variety of ways in West African cuisine. They are eaten alone as a snack and also feature in some West African savoury dishes, such as Ivorian *avocado soup*, as well as *akwaba salad* - mixed greens tossed with Ivorian marinated spices and topped with fresh avocado, tomatoes and boiled eggs.

Nutrition facts:

Avocados are a rich source of monounsaturated fat and omega-3 fatty acids, which reduce the risk of heart disease. They are also very high in potassium, containing three times more potassium than bananas. In addition, they contain fibre and are rich in B vitamins, vitamin E and vitamin K.

Did you know that...?

The avocado contains more protein, fat and calories than any other fruit except the African pear.

Velvet Tamarind (Dialium guineense)

(Also known as Black Tamarind, Black velvet and Tumble tree).

Francophone West Africa: Tamarinier noir.

Nigeria: Ichekwu (Igbo), Tsamiyan biri (Hausa), Awin (Yoruba).

Gambia: Kosito (Mandinka); Solam solam, Solom (Wolof).

Ghana: Osena, Yooye (Twi).

Benin Republic: Assonswen, Asiswetin (Fon), Anwin (Yoruba).

Guinea: Kuyfoytai.

Sierra Leone: Black tumbla.

Contained in a velvety black-brown shell, velvet tamarind fruit is a powdery, pale to rusty orange pulp, surrounding a flat, brown shiny seed. The fruit of the velvet tamarind tree possess a sweet-sour taste, as do its leaves which can also be chewed.

Nutrition facts:

Velvet tamarind fruit are an excellent source of vitamin C, essential for wound-healing and a healthy immune system.

Did you know that...?

In parts of West Africa, twigs from the velvet tamarind tree are used as chewing sticks for oral hygiene. Studies show that they contain anti-microbial compounds which combat the bacteria responsible for plaque formation and dental decay.

Goat Meat

Ghana: Aponkye, Aberikyere (Ashanti).
Nigeria: Anu ewu (Igbo), Ewure (Yoruba), Akuye (Hausa).
Cameroon: Nyama mboli (Bakweri).
Benin Republic: Gbo (Fon), Naa (Bariba), Ogufe (Nagot).

With its own distinct flavour and a texture described as a cross between lamb and beef, goat meat features heavily in West African cuisine. It is an essential ingredient of *goat pepper soup*, a popular appetiser in Nigeria, Liberia and Cameroon. Goat meat is also stewed and eaten roasted or grilled. In Senegal, Benin Republic and Gambia, *brochettes* are a popular snack food consisting of small pieces of goat meat which are skewered and grilled over an open fire.

Nutrition facts:

Goat meat is lower in calories and fat (total and saturated), than lamb, beef and chicken. It is also rich in iron and B vitamins. Due to its lower fat content, goat meat toughens easily, making the protein in it indigestible. It should therefore not be overcooked.

Did you know that...?

Goat meat is fast becoming a gourmet meat. It is now a popular feature on the menus of top restaurants in both London and New York, and for the first time Harrods, one of London's most prestigious food halls, now stocks goat meat.

Guinea Fowl (Numida melagris)

(Also known as Guinea hen).

Francophone West Africa: Pintade.

Nigeria: Zabuwa (Hausa), Ogazi (Igbo), Awo (Yoruba).

Ghana: Akonfem (Twi).

Sierra Leone: Gini, Ginien (Krio).

Cameroon: Kpwai (Bakweri).

This small West African game bird is popular because of its distinct flavour and its dark, delicate meat can be cooked in a variety of ways. In West African cuisine, it is common for guinea fowl to be well-seasoned, then roasted or cooked over a flame-grill. In addition, guinea fowl are known for their high egg-laying capacity and their eggs are often sold hard-boiled in many West African markets.

Nutrition facts:

Guinea fowl is a naturally low-fat source of protein. It is high in B vitamins, including vitamin B_1 (thiamin), which is needed for the continuous release of energy from carbohydrate-containing foods. It is also rich in iron, an essential component of haemoglobin, the red pigment in blood which carries oxygen around the body. Guinea fowl is also a rich source of zinc, which plays a key role in keeping the immune system healthy.

Did you know that...?

Guinea fowl is served in many top restaurants in Europe and is related to pheasant, a popular game bird widely eaten in the UK.

Giant West African Land Snails
(Archachatina marginata)

(Also known as The Big black and Giant snail).

Gambia: Misalingo (Mandinka).

Nigeria: Igbin (Yoruba), Eju (Igbo), Katantawa (Hausa).

Ghana: Nwa (Twi), Waa (Ga), Pobere (Akan), Ahua (Dangme).

Sierra Leone: Konk (Krio).

Liberia: Dain (Nano), Drainn (Gio), Proli (Kpelle).

Burkina Faso &Togo: Kreteke (Hausa).

Cameroon: Nyamangoro (Bakweri), Ko.

Giant West African land snails are a significant and essential part of the diet in many West African countries. They are particularly popular in Nigeria, Ghana and Ivory Coast, where they are considered a delicacy. They are used in soups and stews in these countries and even to make spicy kebabs consisting of seasoned snail meat. In Gambia, they are used to make one of Gambia's most popular rice dishes – *benechin*. Snail meat is also often smoked as a means of preserving it.

Nutrition facts:

Giant West African land snails are an excellent source of protein and iron, and are naturally low in fat. In addition, giant West African land snails contain good amounts of other important minerals such as magnesium, phosphorus, potassium and sodium. They are high in calcium needed for blood clotting, healthy

bones and teeth and also a good source of vitamin A. Despite being low in fat, giant West African land snails contain substantial amounts of essential fatty acids which are needed for good health, but which the body cannot produce.

Did you know that...?

Snail farming is known as heliculture, and on snail farms, giant West African land snails are fed papapya as a means of stimulating their appetite and enabling fast growth. They are also fed palm fruit.

Tropical Periwinkles (Tympanotonus fuscatus)

(Also known as Mangrove periwinkles).

Ghana: Abibia (Twi).

Nigeria: Ikari isam, Imoni isam (Efik); Imekpe (Itsekiri).

Cameroon: Isam.

Liberia: Kiss meat.

Tropical periwinkles are popularly eaten along coastal areas of West Africa, where they are considered a delicacy. Harvested from muddy river beds, there are two types of tropical periwinkle – the *fuscatus* variety, with spikes on its shell and more meat; and the *radula* variety with a smooth shell and less meat. They are used in a range of soups and stews, and are an essential ingredient in *edikaikong*, a soup of the Efik-speaking people of south-eastern Nigeria.

Cleaned and cooked periwinkles are shelled with the aid of a needle before adding to soups. Alternatively, cleaned periwinkles can be cooked in soups in their shells. They can then be sucked straight out of their shells, earning them the name *kiss meat* in Liberia. Cleaned periwinkles can also be roasted in their shells, then shelled and eaten as a snack.

Nutrition facts:

Tropical periwinkles are rich in protein and are a good source of omega-3 fatty acids, which are essential for heart health. Research has shown that they are

also a good source of calcium and an excellent source of iron. Their high iron content most likely explains why tropical periwinkles are eaten to treat anaemia and are a delicacy favoured by pregnant women, who tend to be prone to anaemia.

Did you know that...?

Tropical periwinkle shells are used as chipping for buildings in the West African construction industry. The shells, when ground into a powder, are also used as a source of calcium in animal feeds. If stored in bags and kept moist, freshly harvested tropical periwinkles can survive for three months out of their natural habitat.

Dried Prawns and Shrimps (Macrobrachium and Atya species)

(Also known as African river prawn, Brackish river prawn, Volta river prawn, Gabon shrimp and Ekusa shrimp).

Francophone West Africa: Crevette gros-doigt, Un doigt.

Ghana: Munko (Twi).

Cameroon: Njanga (Bakweri), Ekusa (Soubou).

Nigeria: Ede (Yoruba), Oporo (Igbo).

Senegal: Sipa sipa (Wolof).

Guinea: Sanfoui, Sanson (Soussou).

Ivory Coast: Sanzaket (Appollonia), Abitan (Aboure).

Gabon: Otana.

Liberia: Mesurado shrimp.

Ghana: Osa (Dangme).

Dried prawns and shrimps feature heavily in West African cuisine, especially along the coast. Freshly caught shrimps and prawns are smoked as a means of preservation, resulting in their distinct taste. Used whole, or ground into a powder and added to dishes, they impart a pungent, appetising flavour.

Nutrition facts:

Dried prawns and shrimps contain good levels of zinc, iodine, phosphorous, potassium, selenium and iron, and smaller amounts of magnesium and sodium. They are a very important source of calcium, and an extremely good source of protein, yet are very low in fat and calories, making them a very healthy choice of food. Although prawns and shrimps are high in cholesterol, they do not contribute to high blood cholesterol levels. This is because cholesterol in food does not raise blood cholesterol levels.

Did you know that...?

In Ivory Coast and other Francophone West African countries, the French term for dried shrimps and prawns is 'un doight' (meaning a finger), reflecting their resemblance to human fingers.

Stockfish

Nigeria: Okporoko (Igbo), Panla (Yoruba).

Cameroon: Mokanjo (Bakweri).

Ghana: Kako (Twi).

Traditionally a product of Norway, stockfish is unsalted freshwater fish, (usually cod or a related species). To preserve them, the fish are dried in special drying houses, or sun- and wind-dried on wooden racks called flakes. Prior to drying, they are usually beheaded, split, and gutted. Stockfish has a characteristic strong aroma and taste, and is widely used to add flavour to soups and other West African dishes.

Nutrition facts:

The drying process results in the removal of about 80% of the water in stockfish. However, a good proportion of the nutrients from the fresh fish is retained and these therefore become more concentrated. Consequently, stockfish is rich in protein, vitamin B_1 (thiamin), vitamin B_2 (niacin) and vitamin B_6 (pyridoxine). It also has good amounts of iron and calcium.

Did you know that...?

Norway is the largest producer of stockfish. Known as *torrfisk* or *stokkfisk*, it is considered a national delicacy. Stockfish is also eaten in Italy where it is known as *stoccafisso*.

Bonga Fish (Ethmalosa fimbriata)

(Also known as West African herring and Shad).
Gambia: Challo, Chalyo (Mandinka); Kobo, Oba (Wolof).
Nigeria: Shawa (Yoruba), Azu ikpo (Igbo).
Cameroon: Bonga, Evaka (Bakweri).
Liberia: Bonnie fish, Dried bonnie.
Sierra Leone: Drai Bonga (Krio).

Bonga fish is a tasty, popular fish eaten in many parts of West Africa. It can be used in various forms, including fresh, smoked, salted and dried, and fermented. Smoked bonga fish is the most popular bonga fish product in West Africa, and is used to impart flavour to soups and other West African dishes. Bonga fish is highly sought after in Senegal where fresh, boneless fillets are minced and used in the preparation of *boulettes* (fish balls) and *farci* (stuffed fish).

Nutrition facts:

Bonga fish is a good source of omega-3 fatty acids and protein. When eaten, the bones are a significant source of calcium, phosphorous and fluoride, all of which play an important role in bone and teeth health. Bonga fish also contains iodine, a mineral needed for the production of thyroxine by the thyroid gland.

Did you know that...?

Guinea is the largest producer of smoked bonga fish in West Africa.

Crayfish (Nematopalaemon hastatus)

(Also known as West African Estuarine prawn and White shrimp).
Cameroon: Njanga (Bakweri), Ibanga (Batanga).
Nigeria: Ayiya (Igbo), Ede (Yoruba).
Sierra Leone: Krefis (Krio).

Commonly known in West African English as 'crayfish', these crustaceans are really small prawns that are sun- or smoke-dried. Normally ground into a powder, they are a popular and important West African condiment, imparting a fishy, pungent flavour to various dishes. Crayfish can also be used whole.

Nutrition facts:

Crayfish are low in fat and a good source of protein. They also contain omega-3 fatty acids which are important for heart health and are a significant source of calcium in the West African diet. In addition, crayfish are a source of minerals like selenium, a potent antioxidant, and zinc, which plays an essential role in healing wounds. They also contain potassium, iodine, phosphorous and magnesium.

Did you know that...?

The name Cameroon is said to originate from the Portuguese phrase 'Rio dos Camaroes' (meaning river of prawns), so named by Portuguese explorers who, on their arrival in the 15th century, noticed that river Wouri in Cameroon was swarming with prawns.

Winged Termites (Macrotermes species)

Nigeria: Aku (Igbo), Esunsun (Yoruba), Isekhun (Esan), Khiyea (Hausa).
Liberia: Bug-a-bug.
Ghana: Akenkembe.
Mali: Tu (Dogon).
Senegal: Buloal (Diola).

Winged termites are a popular delicacy in many West African countries. With a delicate, nutty flavour, they make a tasty snack. Usually collected at the beginning of the rainy season, they are washed, lightly salted and gently roasted or dry fried (without oil) until slightly crisp. In Burkina Faso, they are marinated in a salty, dark soy sauce-like mixture, then roasted and served before meals, like an appetiser.

Nutrition facts:

Winged termites are lower in fat and higher in protein than larger livestock meats such as beef, pork and chicken. Additionally, they contain small amounts of high quality fat and are a concentrated source of essential vitamins, especially vitamins B_1 (thiamin) and B_2 (riboflavin), as well as minerals like zinc, copper and iron. Due to their high nutritional value, dry-fried winged termites can be milled into a powder and used to improve the nutritional quality of dishes.

Did you know that...?

There are about two thousand edible insects around the world.

Fonio (Digitaria exilis and Digitaria iburua)

(Also known as Hungry rice and Hungry millet).
Francophone West Africa: Fonio.
Nigeria: Acha, (Hausa), Osikapa acha (Igbo), Suru (Yoruba).
Benin Republic: Podgi (Baatonun).
Ivory Coast: Pom, Pohin (Dan).
Sierra Leone: Fundi (Krio).

Described as one of the world's tastiest cereals, fonio is a popular West African cereal with sand-sized grains. There are two types – white fonio and black fonio, and they are generally eaten as couscous (*djouka* in Burkina Faso, *wusu-wusu* in northern Benin Republic), or as a sweetened yogurt porridge (*degue* in Mali). Fonio has a range of other uses, from brewing beer (*tchapalo* in northern Togo) to making flour for bread-making, to being used as a substitute for semolina.

Nutrition facts:

Fonio is naturally low in fat and has a high protein content. It is particularly high in methionine and cystine, two amino acids vital to human health but not found in many other cereals. Fonio has a low glycaemic index (GI) and is good source of phosphorous and potassium.

Did you know that...?

At present, Guinea is the largest producer of fonio, followed by Nigeria and Mali.

Starchy Porridges and Gruels

(Also known as Pap).

Sierra Leone and Benin Republic: Ogi.

Nigeria: Ogi, Ogi-baba (Yoruba); Akamu (Igbo).

Burkina Faso: Ben-saalga.

Ghana: Koko.

Cameroon: Pap, Akamu.

Similar in consistency to custard, starchy porridges and gruels are served plain, savoury or sweet and can be eaten on their own or as an accompaniment to other dishes. They are made from the fermented starch of a variety of cereals including corn, sorghum, millet and guinea corn. Any of these cereals is soaked in water to ferment, releasing starch from the grains in the process. The starch is allowed to settle, the water drained off and the resulting sediment made into a porridge or gruel in very much the same way as custard. Due to their bland taste, these porridges and gruels are traditionally used as weaning foods.

Plain cornstarch is also made into a thicker consistency, put into moulds or wrapped in leaves when hot and allowed to cool. Known as *agidi* by the Igbo and as *eko* by the Yoruba of Nigeria, the resulting solid gel-like product can be eaten as part of a meal along with a stew or soup. Mixing a tomato-based sauce into plain, cooked cornstarch before wrapping it in leaves, or putting into moulds and allowing to cool makes a savoury version of this dish.

Nutrition facts:

Starchy porridges and gruels are an excellent source of B vitamins and provide modest amounts of energy due to their carbohydrate content.

Did you know that…?

Traditional fermented gruels may have probiotic properties, as they contain *Lactobacillus plantarum*, a microorganism known for its probiotic benefits. Probiotics are helpful bacteria that can improve the health of your gastrointestinal system.

Black-eyed Beans (Vigna unguiculata)

(Also known as Cowpeas).

Francophone West Africa: Haricot.

Gambia: N'ebe, Nyebe (Wolof, Aku); Sep, Sebu (Wolof); Soso (Mandinka).

Senegal: Niebe (Wolof).

Nigeria: Ewa (Yoruba), Agwa (Igbo), Wake (Hausa).

Ghana: Adua (Twi).

Sierra Leone: Binch (Krio).

Benin Republic: Ayikun (Fon).

Cameroon: Ekoki (Bafia), Konn (Ewondo), Wonda m'bale (Douala).

Black-eyed beans, or cowpeas, are the all-important ingredient of a number of popular West African dishes, including bean fritters (*akara* in Nigeria and *niebe beignets* in Senegal and Benin Republic), and one-pot bean stews like Ghanaian *red-red*. Black-eyed beans are also used to prepare a savoury, steamed pudding known as *moin-moin* in Nigeria, *tubani* in Ghana, *koki* or *ekoki* in Cameroon, and *oleleh* in Sierra Leone.

Nutrition facts:

Black-eyed beans are highly nutritious and are a rich source of protein. They also contain minerals like iron, phosphorus, calcium, magnesium, selenium and manganese. In addition, they are a good source of B vitamins as well as fibre. Like other pulses such as soya beans, black-eyed beans have a high soluble fibre content, known to reduce cholesterol levels by acting as a sponge to 'mop up' cholesterol. Their skins are also a great source of insoluble fibre, which is known to prevent constipation and reduce the risk of bowel cancer.

Did you know that...?

Boiling black-eyed beans in salted water actually lengthens their cooking time. This is because added salt hardens the water. The flavour of steamed bean pudding is enhanced by the leaves of the sweet prayer plant (*ketenfe* in Sierra Leone), in which the bean pudding mix is traditionally wrapped prior to steaming. Studies show that this is due to the aromatic oil present in its leaves.

Corn (Zea mays)

Francophone West Africa: Mais.

Nigeria: Masara (Hausa), Oka (Igbo), Agbado (Yoruba).

Ghana: Aburo (Twi).

Gambia: Manyo (Mandinka).

Senegal: Mboq (Wolof).

Sierra Leone: Kohn (Krio).

Cameroon: Mbasi (Douala).

Benin Republic: Gbade (Fon); Igbado, Agbado (Nagot).

A staple in West African cuisine, corn has a variety of uses. It is boiled or roasted on the cob and served as a side dish or snack. It is also ground into corn meal (*lifin* in Togo), which can be cooked into *owo* (a corn meal dough) and eaten with stews and soups. In Ivory Coast, this is known as *to* (pronounced toe). Two important corn-based dishes in Benin Republic are *pate blanche* and *pate rouge*. A similar dish known simply as *pate* is native to Togo.

Additionally, starch from corn is fermented and cooked into a number of popular West African dishes such as *mawe*, a fermented corn dough indigenous to Benin Republic. In Ghana, this is known as *kenkey*, and a version made with added fermented cassava is called *banku*. *Ogi* or *akamu*, a starchy gruel made from fermented corn starch is eaten in Nigeria and is known as *koko* in Ghana. Thick *ogi*, when allowed to cool and set, is known as *agidi* or *eko*, which is eaten with stews or soups. In Benin Republic, this dish is known as *akassa*.

Nutrition facts:

Corn is a great source of fibre and contains good amounts of vitamin C, zinc, magnesium and folic acid. It is also a source of beta-carotene, which the body converts into vitamin A, needed for good vision.

Did you know that...?

Corn is grown on every continent in the world except Antarctica.

Rice (Oryza sativa and Oryza glaberrima Steudel)

Francophone West Africa: Riz.

Cameroon: Erisi (Banyong), Kondi (Bakweri).

Senegal: Ceeb (Wolof).

Nigeria: Shinkafa (Hausa), Osikapa (Igbo), Iresi (Yoruba).

Sierra Leone: Rehs, Fehn-fehn (Krio); Kono, Pa (Temne); Mba, Mbei (Mende).

Gambia: Mano (Mandinka).

Ghana: Omo (Twi).

Rice has a special place in West African cuisine, especially as it is an essential ingredient of *jollof rice*, the most popular rice dish in the region. Additionally, it is considered such an important staple, that in some parts of West Africa (like Sierra Leone), one is considered to not have eaten if they have not had any rice all day. Other West African rice dishes include *malo zaamen*, a popular dish in Burkina Faso, the origin of which may be traced back to *tiebou djen*, the national rice-based dish of Senegal.

Two types of rice are eaten in West Africa – Asian rice *(Oryza sativa)* and African rice *(Oryza glaberrima),* and their use is not limited to just savoury dishes. In Liberia, raw rice is pounded into coarse rice meal and made into *country bread* which is eaten as a snack, while in Sierra Leone, rice meal is mixed with mashed ripe bananas and other ingredients to make Sierra Leonean *rice bread*.

Nutrition facts:

Rice is principally a carbohydrate source but also contains fibre, calcium, iron, and phosphorus, as well as vitamins B_1 (thiamin) and B_3 (niacin). Compared to Asian rice, African rice has greater amounts of all these nutrients except for calcium, because it is more difficult to polish. Asian rice is polished to a greater degree, and therefore more of its nutrients (especially vitamin B_1) are lost.

Did you know that...?

Rice is the second most cultivated grain in the world and is actually a type of grass.

Palm Oil

Nigeria: Mai ja (Hausa), Epo kupa (Yoruba), Mmanu nri (Igbo).
Gambia: Teng' tulo, Tuluseo (Mandinka).
Ghana: Engo (Twi).
Sierra Leone: Pamai (Krio).
Benin Republic: Amivovo, Adinmiwe (Fon), Zomi (Mina).
Cameroon: Mauja, Mbia (Bakweri).

A staple in West African cooking, palm oil is used to flavour and give the well-recognised appetising red colour of many West African dishes, and is the second most largely consumed oil in the world. This rich, red oil is pressed from the fibrous flesh around the nut of palm fruits from the African oil palm tree *(Elaeis guineensis)*. In Liberia, a similar oil is also extracted from fermented palm fruits and is known as *torbogee oil*. Palm fruits (*dekin* in Benin Republic) are popularly used in making *palm fruit soup*, a well-liked West African soup also known as *abenkwan* in Ghana, *palm butter soup* in Liberia, *banga nut soup* in Sierra Leone, *banga soup* in Nigeria and *mbanga soup* in Cameroon.

Palm kernel oil is extracted from the nut of the palm fruit itself and so does not have the flavour or deep red colour. It is much higher in saturated fat than palm oil and is often used in commercially baked products and cosmetics. It is sometimes labelled "palm oil" but should not be confused with the oil extracted from the palm fruit. In many West African countries palm kernel oil is used as a skin moisturiser as well as in cooking.

Nutrition facts:

Palm oil is the richest source of vitamin A and contains fifteen times more beta-carotene than carrots. It is also the richest natural source of a powerful form of vitamin E called tocotrienol, which, according to research can prevent arteriosclerosis and lower cholesterol. Although palm oil gets a bad reputation for being highly saturated (it contains 50% saturated fatty acids), it is actually healthier than palm kernel oil and is also a good source of calcium and phosphorous.

Did you know that...?

With the exception of coconut oil, palm and palm kernel oils are the only vegetable oils that are high in saturated fat. Palmolive soap, a popular brand of soap, is named after palm kernel and olive oils, which are both used in its manufacture.

Egusi Seeds (Citrullus lanatus and Cucumeropsis manii)

(Also known as Egusi melon and White seed melon).

Ghana: Akatsewa (Twi), Neri, Niri, Egushi.

Nigeria: Egusi (Igbo); Agushi (Hausa); Ibara, Egusi bara, Ito (Yoruba).

Liberia: Hingo (Kissi).

Gambia: Aku (Wolof), Sara kulo (Mandinka).

Benin Republic: Egusi bara, Egusi itoo (Tchabe).

Senegal: Beref (Wolof).

Sierra Leone: Ehgusi, Bara (Krio), Henguo (Kissi).

In West Africa, shelled egusi seeds have a number of uses. They are ground into a powder used to thicken soups and stews, or shaped into patties or balls and cooked in soups as a meat substitute. In south-eastern Nigeria, they are roasted together with peanuts and pepper, and ground into an oily paste known as *ose-oji*, which is served as an accompaniment to cola nuts, garden eggs and pepper fruit *(mmimi)*. Fermented egusi seeds are used as a popular condiment known as *ogiri-isi* and *avrouda* in Nigeria and Benin Republic respectively. This condiment is free from both monosodium glutamate (MSG) and salt, making it a much healthier seasoning. Unshelled seeds are boiled and eaten as a snack and oil from egusi seeds is used for cooking, especially in northern Ghana.

Nutrition facts:

Egusi seeds are more than 50% fat, of which 79% is polyunsaturated fat. They are a good quality protein source, and provide significant amounts of vitamins, especially vitamins B_1 (thiamin), B_2 (riboflavin) and B_3 (niacin). They also contain minerals like phosphorus, potassium, magnesium, manganese, sulphur, calcium, iron and zinc, as well as some carbohydrates and small amounts of fibre.

Did you know that...?

Egusi seeds come from the gourd of the egusi plant, a close relative of the water-melon plant.

Dika Nuts (Irvingia gabonensis)

(Also known as African Mango Nuts).

Francophone West Africa: Mangue Savauge.

Nigeria: Apon (Yoruba); Ogbono, Agbono (Igbo); Agwano (Hausa).

Sierra Leone: Bobo.

Benin Republic: Oro Oyibo (Yoruba); Asro, Assrotin (Fon).

Gabon: Andok (Fang).

Ivory Coast: Boboru, Wanini.

Cameroon: Andok, Mbumbwe'bo, Nja'a (Batanga).

Dika nuts are the seeds of the African mango and are best known for their natural thickening ability. They also impart a sharp and spicy aftertaste to soups and sauces. These qualities make them an essential ingredient in *ogbono soup* which is eaten all over West Africa.

Nutrition facts:

Dika nuts are high in polyunsaturated fat and are a good protein source, containing six of the eight essential amino acids. They also contain potassium, calcium and phosphorus, as well as soluble fibre - this has the ability to lower blood cholesterol levels and also regulate blood sugar levels.

Did you know that...?

The slippery consistency produced by milled dika nuts is due to the presence of certain polysaccharides (carbohydrates), which become viscous when heated.

Groundnuts (Arachis hypogaea)

(Also known as Monkey nuts and Peanuts).

Nigeria: Gyada (Hausa), Epa (Yoruba).

Senegal: Gerte (Wolof).

Gambia: Tio, Tiya (Mandinka); Guerte, Gerte (Wolof).

Ghana: Nkate (Twi).

Sierra Leone: Granat (Krio).

Benin Republic: Aziin (Fon).

Cameroon: Ngondo.

Liberia: Groundpeas.

Groundnuts have a myriad of uses in West African cuisine. They are eaten whole (either roasted or boiled) as a snack, or made into peanut butter, a smooth paste and essential ingredient used to thicken *groundnut stew* or soup in Cameroon, Senegal, Cote D'Ivoire, Mali, Ghana and Sierra Leone. Groundnuts are also used to make groundnut oil (*tia tulo* in Gambia), and in south-eastern Nigeria, they are made into a spicy peanut butter (*ose-oji*), served with cola nuts or garden eggs as a sign of welcome or hospitality.

In addition, groundnuts are used in the preparation of a popular, West African meat kebab (*suya* in Nigeria and *chichinga* in Ghana), made from flat pieces of boneless chicken, mutton, beef or goat. The meat is coated with a mix of finely milled groundnut powder (*yaji*), spices, salt and other seasonings, before being skewered, drizzled with vegetable oil, then cooked over or around a glowing fire.

Nutrition facts:

Groundnuts are a rich source of protein and vitamins B_1 (thiamin), B_2 (riboflavin) B_3 (niacin) and B_6 (pyridoxine). They also contain vitamin E, folic acid, good amounts of fibre, and are also a good source of copper, zinc, and iron.

Did you know that...?

Groundnuts are technically a legume and contain more protein than most other nuts. Raw groundnuts contain trypsin inhibitor, a substance which prevents the functioning of trypsin - an enzyme required for the absorption of protein. Trypsin inhibitor is however destroyed by cooking.

Sesame Seeds (Sesamum indicum L)

(Also known as Benniseed, Benne, Sim-sim and Sem-sem).

Gambia: Ogiri (Wolof), Beno (Mandinka).

Sierra Leone: Behni sid, Behni, Ogiri (Krio).

Nigeria: Eluru, Ekuku (Yoruba); Karkashi (Hausa).

Benin Republic: Gusi.

Liberia: Benneseed.

Sesame seeds have a nutty flavour and crunchy texture. They are used to make sesame oil (known as *benne tulo* in Gambia), and are fermented in Sierra Leone to make *ogiri saro,* a condiment very similar to *dawadawa* (fermented locust beans). They are also an important ingredient in *sesame balls*, a Malinese dessert food, and in Liberia, *benneseed paste (*roasted, mashed sesame seeds) is added to *pepper soup* for extra flavour.

Nutrition facts:

Sesame seeds contain vitamins B_1 (thiamin), B_2 (riboflavin) and B_3 (niacin), and are rich in vitamin E and zinc. They are a good source of protein and are exceptionally rich in calcium and iron. They are also high in omega-6 fatty acids.

Did you know that...?

Sesame seeds are thought to have originated in Africa and come in a variety of colours including brown, red, black, yellow and ivory.

Fermented Locust Beans (Parkia biglobosa and Parkia clappertoniana)

Francophone West Africa: Soumbara, Soumbala.

Senegal: Netetou (Wolof), Nyateku.

Nigeria: Dawadawa, Iru (Yoruba); Daddawa (Hausa).

Ghana: Kpalugu, Dawadawa.

Mali: Nere (Bambara).

Gambia: Nettetuo (Wolof), Tulingo (Mandinka), Egelai (Jola).

Sierra Leone: Khinda, Kehnda (Krio).

Benin Republic: Iru (Yoruba), Afitin (Fon), Sonru (Bariba).

Fermented locust beans are a well-known and indispensable condiment throughout West Africa, and are used to enhance and intensify flavour in soups, sauces and other dishes. They are available as blackish balls, or flattened cakes and in soups, provide a nutritious, non-meat protein substitute.

Fermented locust beans possess a characteristic strong, cheesy smell, and one writer has consequently commented that they "sit on the same pedestal as limburger in Europe, fish paste in Indonesia and Vietnam, and Vegemite in Australia". This smell however disappears once the beans are added to cooking. In some parts of Chad, northern Ghana, Mali and Senegal, fermented locust beans are used as an alternative condiment to fermented fish.

Nutrition facts:

Fermented locust beans are a good source of protein, due to free amino acids released during the fermentation process. They are particularly rich in glutamate, an amino acid largely responsible for their flavour-enhancing properties. Unlike monosodium glutamate (MSG), fermented locust beans are low in sodium, which is known to raise blood pressure levels, making them a healthier alternative to MSG-containing condiments. Fermentation also significantly increases the thiamin (vitamin B_1), riboflavin (vitamin B_2) and niacin (vitamin B_3) content of fermented locust beans, making them a significant source of these B vitamins.

Did you know that...?

Sun-dried fermented locust beans can keep for over a year in traditional earthenware pots, without refrigeration. Like stock cubes, fermented locust beans are available in cube form. Marketed under the trade name of *Dadawa* by Cadbury Plc in Nigeria, they are the first and only Nigerian seasoning made from locust beans. Soya beans can also be fermented to make a similar product known as soy-*dawadawa*.

Ogiri

Ogiri is a fermented condiment used to enhance the flavour of soups in many West African countries. There are different versions of this condiment: in Nigeria and Cameroon, it is made from *egusi* seeds, and in Sierra Leone, sesame seeds are used, with the end product known as *ogiri saro*. Also in Nigeria, fluted pumpkin seeds are used to make *ogiri nwan*, while castor oil seeds *(laraa)* are used to make *ogiri Igbo*. In preparing ogiri, the seeds used are usually boiled for about 4 hours and drained once cooled. The drained seeds are then ground into a soft mash which is wrapped tightly in banana leaves and allowed to ferment for a few days. The wrapped ogiri is then treated with smoke as a means of preserving it. Once added to cooking, the strong smell of ogiri disappears.

Nutrition facts:

Ogiri made from egusi seeds is a good source of vegetable protein and B vitamins needed for energy release in the body. It also has a high potassium content and contains smaller amounts of sodium, calcium, magnesium, iron, copper, phosphorous and zinc.

Did you know that...?

Castor oil seeds, which can be used to make ogiri, are ordinarily inedible as they contain recin, a toxic protein, as well as recinine and recinoleic acid, two other toxic substances. These are all removed by the fermentation process.

African Oil Beans (Pentaclethra macrophyllum)

(Also known as Congo acacia, Atta beans and Owala seeds).
Nigeria: Ukpaka, Ugba (Igbo); Kiriya (Hausa); Kohi (Fulani); Okpehe, Okpiye (Edo, Tiv); Ayan (Yoruba).
Sierra Leone: Faewi.
Senegal: Kitao, Kisauda (Banyun).

African oil beans are cooked, processed and fermented into *ugba*, the main ingredient of a quick and easy salad of the same name, favoured amongst the Igbo of south-eastern Nigeria. Often reserved for special occasions, this dish consists of thinly sliced fermented oil beans and a variety of assorted meats and stockfish in a dressing of palm oil, indigenous rock salt, and seasoning. Sliced garden eggs, finely shredded cooked cassava *(abacha)*, and shredded leafy green vegetables, are also included, depending on preference. *Ugba* fermented for less than 3 days is used as a salad ingredient; when fermented for longer it is used as a soup thickener, adding flavour and variety to soups such as *okra soup*.

Nutrition facts:

African oil beans are about 50% fat (consisting mainly of polyunsaturated fatty acids), 23-28% protein, and 20% carbohydrates. Fermentation makes them even more nutritious as amino acids are released from protein during the fermentation process. As such, fermented oil beans are an excellent protein source and contain good amounts of vitamin B_2 (riboflavin), which increases four-fold during the fermentation process.

Did you know that...?

Despite growing on a tree, the African oil bean is actually a legume rather than a seed.

African Pepper (Xylopia aethiopica)

(Also known as Negro pepper, Moor pepper and Ethiopian pepper).

Ghana: Chimba, Kimba, (Hausa); Hwentia, Hwenteaa (Twi).

Guinea: Siminyi (Sousou), Gile-bete (Pulaar).

Guinea Bissau: Malagueta, Malagueta da Guine, Malagueta preta, Pimenta da Guine, Pimenta preta (Crioula).

Ivory Coast: Sindian (Baule).

Liberia: Deo.

Nigeria: Unie (Edo); Ata (Efik); Kimbaa (Hausa); Uda, Oda (Igbo); Eeru, Erunje (Yoruba).

Senegal: Kaani (Mandinka), Ndiar (Wolof).

Sierra Leone: Spaistik (Krio).

Gambia: Kaanifin (Mandinka).

Togo: Sosi (Tem).

Burkina Faso: Guili.

Gabon: Okala, Oyang (Fang).

Cameroon: Achu spice.

These long, brown pods can be used fresh but are often dried before use. During the drying process, African pepper pods are often smoked, resulting in their signature smoky, spicy flavour. African pepper seeds are ground into a powder and used to prepare a spicy fish or meat broth *(pepper soup)*, which is served as an appetiser or as a cure-all medicine for the sick. In south-eastern Nigeria, these pods are an essential ingredient in a similar clear broth prepared for lactating mothers.

Nutrition facts:

African pepper seeds are a good source of vitamins C, B_1 (thiamin), B_2 (riboflavin) and B_3 (niacin), as well as potassium, phosphorus, calcium and magnesium. In addition, they contain small amounts of sodium, zinc, copper and iron. They are also a good source of phytochemicals, which are known to have antioxidant properties and protect the body against free-radical damage.

Did you know that...?

Before the arrival of black peppercorns, African pepper was popularly used in Europe. The Twi name for African pepper literally means 'slender nose' referring to the shape of the fruit pods.

Aidan Tree Fruit Pod (Tetrapleura tetraptera)

Francophone West Africa: Fruit à 4 ailes.
Cameroon: Esekeseke (Bakweri), Eseke (Doula).
Ghana: Prekese (Twi).
Gabon: Enziese.
Nigeria: Osakirisan (Igbo), Aidan-onigun, Aridan (Yoruba);
Uyayak, Edeminyang (Efik); Ikoho (Nupe), Ighimiakia (Edo).
Senegal: Bu seseng (Diola), Busilin (Wolof).

The seeds inside dried Aidan tree fruit pods are used as a spice to flavour food. They are a popular ingredient of a clear soup known as *pepper soup* in south-eastern Nigeria, *yellow soup* in Western Cameroon and *pepe soup* in southern Cameroon. The fruit also has medicinal properties and in many parts of Nigeria, it is used to cure fever, and as an enema for constipation.

Nutrition facts:

Aidan fruit pod seeds are rich in potassium, which is known to lower blood pressure levels - this probably explains their traditional use in regulating the blood pressure of hypertensive patients. Dried fruit pods are also rich in iron, which likely accounts for their use by lactating mothers to regenerate lost blood. Additionally, the fruit pods contain magnesium and phosphorus, as well as phytochemicals in the form of flavanoids, known to protect against free-radical damage. They also have a low sodium content.

Did you know that...?

Aidan tree fruit pods are used locally in Nigeria in pomades and in soaps. In Ghana, eight different products have been developed from the fruits, including tea bags, brandy, chocolate, toffees, baby food, aidan fruit-flavoured biscuits, and aidan fruit-flavoured palm oil.

Scotch Bonnet Pepper (Capsicum chinense)

(Also known as Chilli pepper, Bonney pepper and Congo pepper).
Francophone West Africa: Gros piment.
Nigeria: Ata rodo (Yoruba), Ose otoro (Igbo), Tattasai (Hausa).
Ghana: Moko hwam (Twi).
Sierra Leone: Smohl pehpeh (Krio).
Benin Republic: Takin, Atakin (Fon).
Cameroon: Ijoko.

Probably the most popular pepper throughout West Africa, the fiery scotch bonnet pepper is used in many dishes and in a variety of ways. Scotch bonnet peppers are added whole to stews to give them spice and aroma, or are pureed and added to cooking to give some 'kick' (heat). They are well liked by Ivorians who have a reputation throughout West Africa for liking food with plenty of 'kick'.

Nutrition facts:

Red scotch bonnet peppers contain high amounts of vitamin C and beta-carotene, which the body converts into vitamin A. Yellow and green versions contain considerably less. Scotch bonnet peppers are very high in potassium and contain good amounts of magnesium and iron. Their high vitamin C content can substantially increase the absorption of iron from other ingredients in a meal, such as beans and grains.

Did you know that...?

The fiery sensation of scotch bonnet peppers is caused by capsaicin - a potent chemical that also triggers the brain to produce endorphins, which are natural painkillers that promote a sense of well being. The spicy heat (or capsaicin) level of peppers is measured in Scoville Heat Units (SHU), using a method developed in 1912 by American chemist Wilbur Scoville.

Bird Pepper (Capsicum annum variety aviculare)

(Also known as Devil's pepper and African bird pepper).

Nigeria: Ata wewe (Yoruba), Ose (Igbo), Tattasai (Hausa).

Gambia: Karno, Kano, Karni (Mandinka); Kani (Wolof).

Senegal: Kaani (Wolof).

Ghana: Moko yaya (Twi).

Sierra Leone: Smohl pehpeh (Krio).

Cameroon: Ijoko.

Though small, bird peppers pack a mighty punch or two and are used in West African cooking for their characteristic heat and bite. They are an essential ingredient of *shitor*, a popular Ghanaian hot sauce that is served as an accompaniment to a number of dishes. Bird peppers can be used fresh or dried.

Nutrition facts:

Bird peppers are packed with vitamin A, a potent antioxidant that boosts the immune system. As the pods mature and darken, high quantities of vitamin C are gradually replaced with beta-carotene and capsaicin levels are at their highest. Red versions contain high amounts of vitamin C and beta-carotene, which the body converts into vitamin A. They also contain potassium, magnesium and iron. As with scotch bonnet peppers, their high vitamin C content can substantially

increase the absorption of iron from other ingredients in a meal.

Did you know that...?

The hotness in peppers is not felt by birds because the heat–producing chemical capsaicin specifically targets pain receptors in mammals that are not present in birds. As such, birds are able to eat peppers, no matter how hot.

Tallow Tree Seeds (Detarium species)

Francophone West Africa: Petit detar, Datah ney, Boire.

Benin Republic: Agoulasala (Kotokoli).

Senegal: Detar, Danq, Datax, Ditax (Wolof).

Gambia: Boto (Fula); Ditah, Ditteh (Wolof); Tallo (Mandika).

Burkina Faso: Kagdga (More).

Nigeria: Tsada, Taura (Hausa); Ofo (Igbo); Gatapo (Kanuri).

Mali: Tama koumba (Bambara).

Guinea: Bodo modo (Malinke), Boto boro (Sousou).

Sierra Leone: Talo (Krio).

In many West African countries, tallow tree seeds are milled into a powder used as a traditional emulsifying, flavouring and thickening agent. Oil can be extracted from these seeds and in Gambia, the green fruit around the seeds is eaten.

Nutrition facts:

Tallow tree seeds have an oil content of 7.5% and are very high in calcium, magnesium, iron, and protein. They are also high in soluble fibre, which studies have shown can lower both blood glucose and blood cholesterol levels.

Did you know that...?

Gum extracted from tallow tree seeds is used in the pharmaceutical industry for coating tablets, enabling a sustained release effect.

African Nutmeg (Monodora myristica)

(Also known as Calabash nutmeg and False nutmeg).

Cameroon: Bebeh, Pebe.

Gabon: Fep (Fang).

Ghana: Wedeeaba, Awere-aba (Twi); Ayerewamba (Fante).

Guinea Bissau: Djambadim (Manding-mandinka).

Ivory Coast: Fuin (Baule).

Liberia: Kray-bu (Kru-basa), Gboite (Mende).

Nigeria: Gujiya dan miya (Hausa), Ehuru (Igbo), Ariwo (Yoruba); Gbafilo, Iwo (Itsekiri).

Sierra Leone: Gboite (Mende), Gombewulo.

The rough sandpaper-like seed coat of African nutmeg is grated and used as a substitute for nutmeg, while its inner seed is ground into an aromatic powder used in meat dishes, particularly *pepper soup, a* popular West African appetiser.

Nutrition facts:

African nutmeg is a good source of minerals. It also contains vitamin C, essential for a healthy immune system, as well as B vitamins needed for energy release.

Did you know that...?

African nutmeg was used in Europe as a substitute for European nutmeg in the 16th century. It is also used as an aromatic and stimulating addition to snuff.

Ashanti Pepper (Piper guineense)

(Also known as False cubeb pepper, West African black pepper, Benin pepper, Guinea cubebs and Climbing black pepper).

Francophone West Africa: Poivre des Achantis, Poivre de Guinee, Poivre de la foret, Cubebe.

Gabon: Ondondo andjik (Fang).

Nigeria: Uziza (Igbo); Atariko (Efik); Iyere, Ata iyere (Yoruba).

Cameroon: Black pepper, Jowe, Bush pepper, Pepe.

Gambia: Kanifingo (Mandinka).

Senegal: Fukungen (Diola), Namaku (Bambara).

Benin Republic: Piment pays.

Ghana: Esro wisa (Twi).

Sierra Leone: Siminji (Krio).

This indigenous pepper-like spice is used both as a culinary spice and in West African traditional medicine. It is very popular in Benin Republic, so much so that its name there translates to "pepper of the country". Ashanti pepper seeds look just like black peppercorns but have little tails which distinguish them from the former. They are highly scented, with an additional aroma reminiscent of camphor or cardamom. One writer describes them as having "a characteristic bite that some liken to a turpentine-like aroma."

Nutrition facts:

Ashanti pepper is rich in antioxidants which protect the body against free-radical damage, as well as calcium and phosphorous which are essential for healthy bones and teeth.

Did you know that...?

Ashanti pepper originated in Indonesia and was brought to Africa and the Western world by Arab traders, who used it to season their meat dishes.

Melegueta Pepper (Aframomum melegueta)

(Also known as Alligator pepper, Grains of Paradise and Guinea grains).

Nigeria: Ose oji (Igbo), Atare (Yoruba).

Cameroon: Mbong, Mbongo (Bakweri); Alligator pepe.

Guinea: Kule-kisan (Kissi).

Ghana: Fam wisa (Twi).

Guinea Bissau: Buem-mam, Bu-uma (Mandyak); Breme (Mankanya), Brumbrum (Pepel).

Sierra Leone: Atare (Krio).

Gabon: Ndong (Fang).

Gambia: Sumais (Diola), Belankuto (Mandinka), Suma (Jola).

An indigenous spice, melegueta pepper is similar in appearance and flavour to cardamom seeds with a pungent, peppery taste. These small, spicy, reddish-brown seeds grow in large pods which are a deep pinkish-red when ripe. After being harvested, the pods are left to dry, and turn dark brown. In addition to being an important ingredient in traditional cooking, melegueta pepper is used as a spicy masticatory in some West African cultures and, along with cola nuts, it is offered to guests as a sign of peace and hospitality.

Nutrition facts:

Melegueta pepper is rich in antioxidants that protect the body against free-radical damage which is associated with the development of some chronic diseases including stroke, diabetes and heart disease. It also contains small amounts of minerals including iron, calcium and phosphorous.

Did you know that...?

Melegueta pepper used to be traded along the West African coast along the Gulf of Guinea from Congo to Sierra Leone. As such, that region became known as the "Pepper coast" or "Grain coast".

Ginger (Zingiber officinale)

Francophone West Africa: Gingembre
Gambia: Nyameo, Nyamayo (Mandinka); Guiyar (Wolof).
Ghana: Akekaduro (Twi).
Nigeria: Atare (Yoruba), Jinja (Igbo).
Sierra Leone: Jinja (Krio).

One of the oldest and more popular medicinal spices, ginger is widely used in West Africa. This root spice is used as an ingredient in a number of dishes such as *jollof rice,* peanut stew (*mafe* in Senegal and Mali; *nkatenkwan* in Ghana), and *chofi*, chargrilled turkey tail seasoned with onions, chilli and ginger .

A variety of distinctive West African beverages are prepared with ginger, including what Ivorians call *gnamakudji*, or ginger juice, often made from crushed ginger mixed with sugar and lemon juice. Some versions use ginger shoots or pineapple skin, steeped in ginger and water, and pineapple juice can be used in place of lemon juice. *Djinimbere,* a similar sweet lemon and ginger drink is commonly served at weddings in Mali. This drink is known as *lemburujii* in Burkina Faso and *gingembre* in Senegal and Gambia.

In Ghana, ginger is also used to make ginger beer as well as *ahomka*, traditional boiled sweets. Consisting of ginger, sugar and other spices, these traditional sweets are said to clear the sinuses in milliseconds.

Nutrition facts:

Ginger contains potassium, magnesium, copper, manganese and vitamin B_6 (pyridoxine). In addition, it contains volatile oils as well as phenols, which are plant substances that have protective properties.

Did you know that...?

Ginger can lessen the symptoms of nausea and motion sickness.

Horse Eye Beans (Mucuna solanei and Mucuna urens)

(Also known as Hamburger bean).

Francophone West Africa: Eil de bourrique.

Sierra Leone: Osyai binch (Krio).

Horse eye beans require considerable care in their preparation due to the toxic substance they contain. Sun-dried, milled horse eye beans are used in small quantities as a soup thickener in eastern Nigeria; in other parts of Nigeria, they are used whole as a substitute for black-eyed beans. In Guinea, horse eye beans are used to make *ragout* (a thick, rich stew), porridge, and even coffee.

Nutrition facts:

Horse eye beans are rich in protein and have an oil content of between 7-23%. They naturally contain toxic levels of the amino acid L-dopa (levodopa), which stimulates the formation of the neurotransmitter dopamine in the brain. They are also a source of minerals, especially potassium, magnesium, calcium and iron.

Did you know that...?

Horse eye beans are a source of L-dopa which is used to treat Parkinson's disease. They also contain a black dye which is used in Nigeria to dye leather. Oil extracted from the beans can be used in the preparation of resin, paint, polish, wood varnish, skin cream and liquid soap.

African Mahogany Beans (Afzelia africana and Afzelia bella)

(Also known as Counterwood tree seeds and African oak seeds).

Nigeria: Akpalata (Igbo), Kawo, Apa (Yoruba); Gayoki (Hausa).

Ghana: Okorosa (Twi), Papao.

Togo: Kpa-kpa.

Sierra Leone: Kontah (Temne).

Benin Republic: Kaluma.

Liberia: Glegoniangaglu (Dan).

Ivory Coast: Azodau (Abe), Lingue.

African mahogany beans are potentially poisonous, but following careful processing they are milled and used to thicken soups in parts of West Africa.

Nutrition facts:

African mahogany beans are a good source of protein and soluble fibre, and are relatively high in iron, zinc and phosphorus. In addition, they contain exceptionally high amounts of calcium (338mg per 100g of beans), which is essential for strong bones and teeth, and can lower high blood pressure levels.

Did you know that...?

The soluble fibre in African mahogany beans has been shown to help normalize and improve blood sugar levels in patients with tablet-controlled Type 2 diabetes.

Spicy Cedar Seeds (Beilschmiedia mannii and Tylostemon mannii)

Francophone West Africa: Cedre epice, Laurier.

Ivory Coast: Attiokwo.

Liberia: Kanda, Pink kanda.

Guinea: Labi (Fula- pulaar), Tola (Susu).

Sierra Leone: Tola (Krio), Angba (Temne); Kpa, Gba (Mende).

Nigeria: Gbako nisa.

The oil-rich seeds of the spicy cedar tree are particularly popular in Sierra Leone, where they are added as a condiment to enrich soups. Known as *tola*, the seeds are roasted, ground and used as a substitute for dried, powdered okra. In Liberia, spicy cedar flowers are commonly used to flavour rice and other food. Additionally, the fruit surrounding the seeds is eaten and used as an ingredient in sauces. Spicy cedar seeds are also popular in Ivory Coast.

Nutrition facts:

Spicy cedar seeds are a good source of calcium and contain phosphorous, both important minerals for building and maintaining healthy bones and teeth.

Did you know that...?

Spicy cedar trees are part of the same family as avocado and bay leaf trees.

Cloves (Eugenia caryophyllata)

Ghana: Prekomama (Akan-wasa), Kanumfari (Fula-fulde).

Mali: Qernfel (Arabic).

Sierra Leone: Aiminii (Krio).

Gambia: Samareo (Mandinka).

Cloves are a versatile spice used in drinks and in sweet and savoury dishes. They are the dried flower buds of an evergreen tree native to eastern Indonesia, and are used in small amounts due to their strong pungent flavour.

Nutrition facts:

Cloves contain dietary fibre, vitamins C and K, and minerals like manganese, iron, magnesium and calcium. They also contain phytochemicals, which are plant substances with antioxidant properties.

Did you know that...?

The island of Pemba in East Africa is famed for its clove honey which is produced by bees that eat nectar from clove flowers.

Black Timber Tree Seeds (Brachystegia eurycoma)

Francophone West Africa: Bobinga, Bois du rose.

Cameroon: Ekop naga.

Ivory Coast: Meblo.

Gabon: Mendou.

Sierra Leone: Bogdei.

Nigeria: Okwe, Achi (Igbo); Ojiji itakun (Yoruba); Okung (Efik).

Liberia: Tebako.

The protein-rich seeds of the black timber tree are ground and used as a thickener in soups. They are especially popular with the Igbo of south-eastern Nigeria, where they are known as *achi* and are used to thicken a soup of the same name.

Nutrition facts:

Black timber tree seeds are rich in carbohydrates and are a significant protein source. They also contain some fat.

Did you know that...?

Though called seeds, black timber tree seeds are actually a type of legume.

Country Onion (Afrostyrax lepidophyllus)

(Also known as Garlic bark tree and Bush onion).
Francophone West Africa: Oignon de pays.
Cameroon: Ngakanga (Bakweri).
Gabon: Essun (Fang).

Country onions, or the seeds of the *Afrostyrax lepidophyllus* tree, have an amazingly distinctive aroma similar to a blend of onions and garlic. A popular spice in Cameroon, the dry seeds are ground into a fine powder which is used in cooking. Due to the strong aroma which pervades the entire country onion tree, its dried tree bark is grated and also used as flavouring. Country onion is at its best when used to flavour fish, but is versatile enough to be used to flavour other dishes.

Nutrition facts:

Country onions are rich in antioxidants, which are proven to prevent free-radical damage. Free-radical damage has been associated with the development of a number of diseases, including diabetes and stroke.

Did you know that...?

It is said that country onions help 'calm' the stomach and so prevent the flatulence usually associated with eating legume-based dishes.

African Nut Tree Seeds

(Also known as African wood-oil nut tree seeds).
Cameroon: Ndjansanga (Bakweri), Njansang (Banka/Bassa).
Benin Republic: Ookwe, Okwen.
Ivory Coast: Akpi, Akin, Akporo (Baule); Eho (Abe).
Gabon: Essessang (Fang), Mughele (Bapounou).
Nigeria: Okwe (Igbo), Erinmado (Yoruba), Nsasana (Efik).
Sierra Leone: Gbolei, Kpolei (Mende); Gbo, Kpo (Kissi).

The oily seeds of the African nut tree *(Ricinodendron heudelotii)* have a characteristic strong, aromatic flavour and a slightly bitter aftertaste. As such, they are a popular spice and soup thickener in many parts of West Africa, working well with fish, chicken and vegetables. Cooking oil is also extracted from them.

Nutrition facts:

African nut tree seeds are rich in calcium, protein and in fat - consisting mainly of unsaturated fat, especially linoleic fatty acids, which may help lower blood cholesterol and reduce the risk of blood clot formation in blood vessels. The seed oil also contains vitamin E (alpha-tocopherol), a potent antioxidant.

Did you know that...?

The bark of the African nut tree is used to treat a range of conditions including cough, leprosy, dysentery, diarrhoea, anaemia, malaria and skin diseases.

Wild Basil (Ocimum gratissimum)

(Also known as Tea bush, Bush basil and Fever plant).

Francophone West Africa: Menthe sauvage; Basilic de Ceylan.

Nigera: Nchuanwu (Igbo), Efirin-nla (Yoruba), Kirare (Hausa).

Sierra Leone: An-gbonto.

Guinea Bissau: Do (Crloulo).

Ghana: Onunum (Twi).

Sengal: Tibus (Wolof), Doreda (Crioula).

Benin Republic: Tchaayo, Gbodoglin (Fon).

The fragrant leaves of the wild basil plant are used as a herb to season meat dishes as well as soups. They are also made into an infusion which is drunk for medicinal purposes, and are an important ingredient for a special broth prepared for breastfeeding mothers in south-eastern Nigeria.

Nutrition facts:

Wild basil contains small amounts of calcium, potassium and magnesium, as well as protein, carbohydrate and fats. It is also a source of phytocehmicals, known to have antioxidant properties.

Did you know that...?

In Benin Republic, and some other parts of West Africa, the wild basil plant is used as an antibiotic to treat wounds.

Utazi (Gongronema latifolium and Marsdenia latifolia

Ghana: Aborode-aborode (Akan-Asante).

Nigeria: Utazi (Igbo), Arokeke (Yoruba).

Senegal: Gasub (Serer).

Sierra Leone: Ndondo-polole (Kissi); Rope quiah (Krio); Buli-yeyako, Nyiya yeyako, Tawa-bembe, Yonigbagboi (Mende); Ra-bilong (Temne).

The shiny pale or dark green leaves of this well-known herb are known for the bitter taste they impart to soups and stews. They are also eaten raw as a salad vegetable and are a popular ingredient in *pepper soup*, into which small amounts are added for flavour.

Nutrition facts:

Utazi leaves are a good source of protein, providing 27g of protein per 100g of leaves. They also have a significant fat content of 18.8g per 100g. They contain good amounts of minerals such as sodium, potassium, calcium, magnesium and especially iron. Research has highlighted the blood glucose-lowering properties of utazi leaf extract, which accounts for its use in traditional medicine as a treatment for diabetes. Utazi leaf extract has also been shown to have lipid-lowering, antioxidant and anti-inflammatory properties.

Did you know that...?

Utazi leaves are traditionally used in controlling weight gain in breastfeeding women, and are said to aid pregnancy.

Cola Nut (Kola nitida and Cola acimuta)

(Also known as Kola Nut, African Cola Nut and Goora Nut).

Nigeria: Oji (Igbo), Obi (Yoruba), Goro (Hausa).

Ghana: Bese (Twi).

Gabon: Wali (Fang).

Senegal: Guro (Wolof).

Sierra Leone: Kola (Krio).

Benin Republic: Vi, Ahowe (Fon).

Cameroon: Kola, Atara (Bakweri).

A popular feature in West African culture, cola nuts play an important role and are commonly used in a ceremonial capacity. For example, they are offered to guests as a sign of hospitality and peace, or offered as gifts to show respect. They are also popular for their stimulant properties especially amongst the Hausa-speaking tribes of West Africa who eat them to dispel sleep and thirst, and to suppress appetite. Cola nuts have an initial bitter taste, followed by a sweet aftertaste.

Nutrition facts:

Cola nuts have a high caffeine and theobromine content, which account for their stimulant properties. They are also high potassium, which is known to help reduce blood pressure levels, and phosphorous which is essential for teeth and bone health. Cola nuts also contain small amounts of iron, magnesium and

calcium.

Did you know that...?

Before the development of synthetic flavourings, cola nuts were used to flavour
carbonated drinks such as Coca-Cola.

Cow Feet

Nigeria: Ukwu anu (Igbo), Ese eran, Bokotor (Yoruba).
Sierra Leone: Kaufut (Krio).
Senegal: Yeilee nakk (Wolof).
Gambia: Ailee nakk (Wolof).

Cow feet are a well-liked delicacy in a number of West African countries, including Liberia, Senegal and Nigeria, where they are boiled till soft. In Nigeria, cow feet are the main ingredient in *nkwobi*, a popular Igbo dish. Cow skin is another popular delicacy in Nigeria where it is called *pomo* or *kanda*. Cow feet are also the basis of Gambian *cow foot pepper soup*, a spicy soup consisting of soft-boiled cow feet, stock and some root vegetables.

Nutrition facts:

Cooked cow feet contain saturated fat and are high in gelatin. Gelatin is an imperfect protein made from collagen and cannot be used to build body tissues by itself. Also, it does not have any nutrients attached to the calories it contains. Its one benefit is that it acts as a protein sparer, enabling the body to use better quality dietary protein more efficiently. Cow feet should therefore not be used as a primary protein source but rather to add variety. They are best eaten with sources of better quality protein, such as meat, fish, poultry or pulses and legumes. The same applies to cow skin, which also has a high collagen content and, when cooked, becomes high in gelatin.

Did you know that...?

Cow feet are eaten in other parts of the world, such as in Mexico and the Caribbean. The feet of young cows is used to make calves' feet jelly, a Jewish delicacy. Cow feet are also used commercially to produce gelatin which is used to make binders for improving the crispness of banknotes.

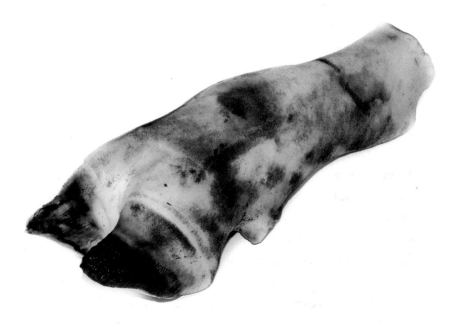

Indigenous Rock Salt

(Also known as Trona and Local salt).

Gambia: Lubi (Wolof).

Nigeria: Akanwu (Igbo), Kaun (Yoruba).

Ghana: Kawo, Kawe (Twi).

Sierra Leone: Lubi (Krio).

Cameroon: Kanwa, Kangwa.

Liberia: Country soda.

Small pieces of indigenous rock salt are used in West African cuisine to give flavour to stews, soups and other dishes. It should not be confused with *potash*, a traditional salt made from the ashes of oil palm and baobab trees. Indigenous rock salt has alkaline properties and is used to emulsify (i.e. bind) oil and water in some West African dishes, such as Nigerian African oil bean salad *(ugba)* and Cameroonian *achu soup*. Additionally, it is traditionally used to tenderise and reduce the cooking time of foods such as beans, meat and stockfish.

The thickening effect of okra and jute *(ewedu)* in soups is enhanced when indigenous rock salt is added to them. In the absence of indigenous rock salt, sodium bicarbonate is often used as a substitute.

Nutrition facts:

Indigenous rock salt is a naturally-occurring sodium carbonate in the form of sodium sesquicarbonate $(Na_2CO_3.NaHCO_3.2H_2O)$, and is therefore high in sodium just like table salt. As such, it should be used in small amounts as a high intake of sodium is known to increase the risk of high blood pressure and therefore strokes.

Did you know that...?

Adding indigenous rock salt to vegetables and beans during cooking actually destroys the vitamin content of these foods and can also reduce the amount of iron available for absorption from them.

Palm Wine

Francophone West Africa: Vin de Palme.

Nigeria: Pami (Igbo); Emu, Oguro (Yoruba).

Ghana: Nsafufuo.

Sierra Leone: Pamwain, Mampana (Krio); Tokpo-lu (Mende).

Gambia: Teng'dolo (Mandinka).

Gabon: Molorolla.

Guinea: Gunuk.

Cameroon: Matango, Mimba (Bakweri), Pami.

Palm wine is the fermented sugary sap of the oil palm (*Elaeis guineense*) and raphia palm (*Raphia hookeri* or *Raphia vinifera*). It is consumed either sweet (slightly fermented), or as a sour, vinegary alcoholic drink. Additionally, palm wine is distilled into a highly alcoholic drink known as *local gin* (*sodabe* in Togo, *kaikai* or *ogogoro* in Nigeria and *akpeteshie* in Ghana).

Palm wine has a very short shelf-life and is at its best when freshly collected. Once collected, it immediately starts to undergo rapid natural fermentation, resulting in increased alcohol levels. The bark of the bitter bark tree (*blundi* in Senegal), is sometimes added to palm wine to prolong its shelf-life. This bark contains chemical compounds which have antimicrobial properties, preventing further fermentation.

Nutrition facts:

Due to fermentation, palm wine is a good source of vitamins B_1 (thiamin), B_2 (riboflavin), B_3 (niacin) and B_6 (pyridoxine), all of which play an important role in the release of energy in the body.

Did you know that...?

In West Africa, palm wine is used as a raising agent in large-scale baking because it contains *Saccharomyces cerevisia*, the yeast responsible for the fermentation process in palm wine. During baking, any alcohol evaporates.

Pigs' Feet

(Also known as Trotters and Hog feet).

Ghana: Prakontwere (Twi).

Sierra Leone: Ogfut (Krio).

Nigeria: Ese elede (Yoruba), Ukwu ezi (Igbo).

Pigs' feet (or trotters) are the cooked feet and ankles of a pig and are very popular in Ghana, Sierra Leone and Liberia, where they are used in a variety of dishes. Due to their sinewy and bony nature, they are cooked slowly for long periods in soups and stews. In Ghana, salted pigs' feet feature in a number of dishes including *pigs' feet stew*. Pigs' feet are also used in the Liberian version of *jollof* rice and to add flavour to Liberian vegetable dishes.

Nutrition facts:

Despite their use in West African cuisine as a meat, pigs' feet are very high in fat, especially saturated fat, which is known to raise cholesterol levels and therefore the risk of heart disease. Consequently, they should be eaten occasionally. Additionally, salted pigs' feet are high in sodium which has been implicated in the development of high blood pressure and stroke. During cooking, the collagen (connective tissue) in pigs' feet is converted into gelatin - a protein with little nutritional value, as it is deficient in essential amino acids that the body cannot produce. That said, gelatin does have the benefit of being a protein sparer, in that it acts as an energy source, enabling the body to use other better quality proteins to build or repair body tissue. Nutritionally speaking, pigs' feet provide most value when used for homemade stocks. When cooled and skimmed of fat, these stocks make a beneficial addition to stews and soups, especially when, during preparation, small amounts of vinegar or lemon juice are added to extract minerals such as calcium, and magnesium from the bones.

Did you know that...?
Pigs' feet are eaten not only in West Africa, but also in Ireland, China, Poland and southern parts of the United States.

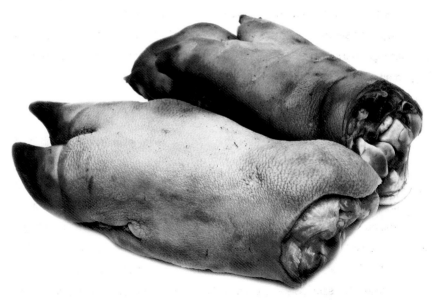

Index